AT THE WILL
OF THE BODY

Arthur W. Frank

AT THE WILL
OF THE BODY

Reflections on Illness

HOUGHTON MIFFLIN COMPANY
Boston/New York

For information about permission to reproduce selections from
this book, write to Permissions, Houghton Mifflin Company,
215 Park Avenue South, New York, New York 10003.

Library of Congress Cataloging-in-Publication Data

Frank, Arthur W.
At the will of the body : reflections on illness /
Arthur W. Frank.
p.   cm.
ISBN 0-395-56188-4   ISBN 0-395-62430-4 (pbk.)
1. Frank, Arthur W. — Health.   2.   Cancer — Patients —
United States — Biography.   3.   Heart — Infarction —
Patients — United States — Biography.   4.   Sick —
Psychology.   I.   Title.
RC265.6.F73A3   1991
616'.001'9 — dc20   90-4459
[B]   CIP

Printed in the United States of America

AGM 10 9 8 7

The quotation from *The Illness Narratives*, by Arthur Kleinman,
M.D., copyright © 1988 by Basic Books, Inc., is reprinted by
permission of Basic Books, Inc., Publishers, New York. The quotation from *Diary of a Zen Nun*, by Nan Shin, © 1986, is reprinted by permission of E. P. Dutton, Inc. The quotation from
"Author's Notes to *The Marriage of Bette and Boo*," by Christopher Durang, published by Dramatists Play Service, is reprinted
by permission of the author. The lyrics from "The Boy in the
Bubble" and "Crazy Love," copyright © 1986 Paul Simon, are
reprinted by permission of Paul Simon Music. The lines from
"Gravy," by Raymond Carver, are from the book *A New Path to
the Waterfall*, copyright © 1989 by the estate of Raymond Carver,
and are used by permission of Atlantic Monthly Press. The lines
from *Tao Te Ching*, by Lao Tzu, translated by Stephen Mitchell,
copyright © 1988 by Stephen Mitchell, are reprinted by permission of HarperCollins Publishers.

To Cathie,

who joins me in remembering

LAURA IRENE FOOTE

1928–1988

and

BARBARA ANN WANNER

1942–1988

ACKNOWLEDGMENTS

Many people influenced this book. I thank them for what they have been to me, but I limit myself to naming those who directly affected the manuscript. My agent, Doe Coover, anticipated what the project was about and helped me hold onto my sense of purpose. The editorial care of Henry Ferris, of Houghton Mifflin, is apparent in every paragraph, if not every line. Peg Anderson, my manuscript editor, clarified my thoughts and intentions throughout. My thanks also to Larry Platt for his assistance with the book's production.

What I know of illness I have learned together with my wife, Catherine Foote. This is our book, no less than they were our illnesses.

CONTENTS

It is possible to talk with patients, even those who are most distressed, about the actual experience of illness. . . . Witnessing and helping to order that experience can be of therapeutic value.

Arthur Kleinman, The Illness Narratives

And someone else wrote me, "What I want is to know your own experience of illness."
    Why the interest?
    People on their ailments are not always interesting, far from it. But we all hope for a — must I say the word — recipe, we all believe, however much we know we shouldn't, that maybe somebody's got that recipe and can show us how not to be sick, suffer and die.

Nan Shin, Diary of a Zen Nun: Every Day Living

Unless you go through all the genuine angers you feel, both justified and unjustified, the feelings of love that you do have will not have any legitimate base and will be at least partially false. Plus, eventually you will go crazy.

Christopher Durang, "Author's Notes to
The Marriage of Bette and Boo"

Illness as a
Dangerous Opportunity

I HAVE EXPERIENCED life-threatening illness twice. I had a heart attack when I was thirty-nine and cancer at age forty. Now that these illnesses are in remission, why go back and write about them? Because illness is an opportunity, though a dangerous one. To seize this opportunity I need to remain with illness a little longer and share what I have learned through it.

Critical illness offers the experience of being taken to the threshold of life, from which you can see where your life could end. From that vantage point you are both forced and allowed to think in new ways about the value of your life. Alive but detached from everyday living, you can finally stop to consider why you live as you have and what future you would like, if any future is possible. Illness takes away parts of your life, but in doing so it gives you the opportunity to choose the life you will lead, as opposed to living out the one you have simply accumulated over the years.

The most obvious danger of disease is that you will continue over the threshold and die. This danger is paramount, and at

Agree hope for better life

some time it will be unavoidable. The danger you can avoid is that of becoming attached to illness, using it to withdraw from encountering yourself and others. Illness is something to recover from if you can, but recovery is worth only as much as what you learn about the life you are regaining.

Recovery has different meanings. After my heart attack it meant putting the whole experience behind me. I wanted to return to a place in the healthy mainstream as if nothing had happened. Cancer does not allow that version of recovery. I am reminded, every time I see a doctor or fill out an insurance form, that there is no "cure" for cancer, only remission. But more important than the physiology of the disease is the impact of the experience. After cancer I had no desire to go back to where I was before. The opportunity for change had been purchased at too great a cost to let it slip away. I had seen too much suffering from a perspective that is often invisible to the young and the healthy. I could not take up the same game in the old terms. I wanted less to recover what I had been than to discover what else I might be. Writing is part of this discovery.

depressing

A problem with the view of recovery as the ideal ending of illness is that some people do not recover. Soon after my treatment for cancer ended, my wife, Cathie, and I returned to the cancer center to be with her mother, whose illness ended in her death at fifty-nine. If recovery is taken to be the ideal, how is it possible to find value in the experience of an illness that either lingers on as chronic or ends in death? The answer seems to be in focusing less on recovery and more on renewal. Even continuing illness and dying contain opportunities for renewal.

To seize the opportunities offered by illness, we must live illness actively: we must think about it and talk about it, and some, like me, must write about it. Through thinking, talking, and writing we can begin, as individuals and as a society, to accept illness fully. Only then can we learn that it is nothing special. Being ill is just another way of living, but by the time we have lived through illness we are living differently. Because illness can lead us to live differently, accepting it is neither easy nor self-evident. I write about illness to work out some terms in which it can be accepted. I want to enter into the experience of illness and witness its possibilities, but not so far as to become attached to being ill. Seizing the opportunity means experiencing it fully, then letting go and moving on.

This book began during my illnesses in conversations and in letters. Of all the care Cathie gave me, the most important was her willingness and ability to talk about what was happening to me and to her. Through our talk illness did not happen just to me, it happened to us. My sense of being part of a larger "us" developed in letters I exchanged with friends and relatives, some of whom had been critically ill themselves. The circle expanded to books by others about their illnesses. Ultimately, as in all experience, no clear line marks off what is "mine" from what I have lived through others.

One letter in particular gave me the start I needed to write this book. A cousin asked me to write to a friend of hers, a man who had lung cancer. Writing to someone you do not know about something as personal as cancer is not easy. But I knew how much it had meant to me, when I was ill, to receive letters from persons willing to become involved in my experience and offering their own experiences to me. When I finally wrote the letter to my cousin's friend, I realized it only hinted at topics needing much more discussion.

I want what I have written to be touched as one touches letters, folding and refolding them, responding to them. I hope ill persons will talk back to what I have written. Talking back is how we find our own experiences in a story someone else has written. The story I tell is my own, but readers can add their lives to mine and change what I have written to fit their own situations. These changes can become a conversation between us.

Too many ill persons are deprived of conversation. Too many believe they cannot talk about their illness. By talk about illness, I do not mean explanations of their diagnoses and treatment. What most ill persons say about their illness comes from their physicians and other medical staff, not from themselves. The ill person as patient is simply repeating what has been said elsewhere — boring second-hand medical talk. When ill persons try to talk in medicalese, they deny themselves the drama of their personal experience.

Ill persons have a great deal to say for themselves, but rarely do I hear them talk about their hopes and fears, about what it is like to be in pain, about what sense they make of suffering and the prospect of death. Because such talk embarrasses us, we do not have practice with it. Lacking practice, we find such talk difficult. People then believe that illness is not something to talk about. They miss the opportunity of learning to experience it with another. Renewal is easiest if it is a shared process.

What I have to tell relates no cures I have discovered or medical miracles. I got sick, went through the prescribed treatments, engaged in my share of obnoxious behavior, managed to cope, and lived to tell the tale. This tale will not tell anyone how to cope, but it does bear witness to what goes into coping. That witness, I believe, is enough.

I am not an inspiring case, only a writer. By profession I am a university professor, a sociologist with additional training and experience in philosophy, communications, and psychotherapy. These resources helped me put my experiences into words. But I do not write as any kind of expert; I present myself only as a fellow sufferer, trying to make sense of my own illness. If I sometimes seem to offer advice, it is only that I am being carried away in my attempt to share experience. I cannot tell people how to be sick any more than I can say how to get well. I can only witness some of the realities of illness.

This book offers starting points for talking and thinking about illness. My own experiences are in no sense a recipe for what others can expect or should experience. I know of no exemplary way to be ill. We all have to find our own way, but we do not necessarily have to be alone. I can write about where I encountered problems and where I found moments of value. Ill persons can hold out these examples of illness experience to family, friends, and medical staff as proof of all there is to talk about. Talk is not the only way to elevate illness beyond pain and loss, but for most people it may be the most reliable way. For those who read this book alone, I hope it will be a good partner in silent conversation. I hope that for most it will be the beginning of conversation with others.

I write first to those who are now ill, but not just to them. Since we all will become ill someday, other readers may find this book useful as a way of considering what that will mean.

I write also to those who care for the ill. Caregivers are the other halves of the conversations I encourage the ill to engage in. They are also the other halves of illness experiences. The care they give begins by doing things for ill persons, but it turns into sharing the life they lead. I hope I suggest something of what there is to be shared.

Since my own experience comprises heart attack and cancer, I write about these illnesses. Cancer gets more attention, not only because my experiences were more extensive, but because social attitudes toward cancer are more complex. Despite this focus, I hope readers experiencing or concerned with other illnesses will not feel excluded. Different diseases set in place different possibilities, but there remains a common core of what critical illness does to a life.

Critical illness leaves no aspect of life untouched. The hospitals and other special places we have constructed for critically ill persons have created the illusion that by sealing off the ill person from those who are healthy, we can also seal off the illness in that ill person's life. This illusion is dangerous. Your relationships, your work, your sense of who you are and who you might become, your sense of what life is and ought to be — these all change, and the change is terrifying. Twice, as I realized how ill I was, I saw these changes coming and was overwhelmed by them.

So I write to the younger self I was before illness overwhelmed me. I write to a self not so many years younger but a gulf of experience away. In a short story by Jorge Luis Borges, the writer, now old, is sitting by a river. Along comes his younger self, out for a walk. They recognize each other and talk. The younger man is particularly shocked that the other is almost blind. The older man comforts him, telling him the condition is nothing to be feared. If my younger self met me now and heard what was to be his medical history, he would be even more shocked than Borges's younger self. In what follows I want to tell my self-before-illness that his fears are legitimate, but he would be a fool to spend his life being fearful. He will suffer and have losses, but suffering and loss are not incompatible with life.

For all you lose, you have an opportunity to gain: closer relationships, more poignant appreciations, clarified values. You are entitled to mourn what you can no longer be, but do not let this mourning obscure your sense of what you can become. You are embarking on a dangerous opportunity. Do not curse your fate; count your possibilities.

Becoming Ill

ONE DAY my body broke down, forcing me to ask, in fear and frustration, what's happening to me? Becoming ill is asking that question. The problem is that as soon as the body forces the question upon the mind, the medical profession answers by naming a disease. This answer is useful enough for practicing medicine, but medicine has its limits.

Medicine has done well with my body, and I am grateful. But doing *with* the body is only part of what needs to be done *for* the person. What happens when my body breaks down happens not just to that body but also to my life, which is lived in that body. When the body breaks down, so does the life. Even when medicine can fix the body, that doesn't always put the life back together again. Medicine can diagnose and treat the breakdown, but sometimes so much fear and frustration have been aroused in the ill person that fixing the breakdown does not quiet them. At those times the experience of illness goes beyond the limits of medicine.

The day I had a heart attack I could not imagine that my body was breaking down. I was thirty-nine years old and thinking about competing in a race the next day. It would be the first race of my tenth year of competitive recreational running. For much of the winter I had had a virus, but it was March, spring was beginning, and last week's cold seemed to be over. I went for a jog along the river behind our house. I was running easily, but my pulse seemed too fast. Passing a parking lot, I saw another runner getting out of his car and took the excuse to stop and talk. I leaned on the hood of his car, started to say something about my heart beating fast, and then woke up on the ground.

Shocked that healthy person had this happen

I had undergone what cardiologists would later call ventricular tachycardia. Simply put, my heart had sped up, beating erratically and uncontrollably fast, then had stopped for a moment. A year later my cardiologist would tell me I was lucky that my heart had started again and that it had not stopped long enough to cause permanent damage. But at the time I did not know what had happened. I had a scraped shin, and I felt shaky.

I got a ride home, took a shower, and that night I even went to a party. I was worried because I had never passed out before, but how serious could it be? I was an athlete, even if a middle-aged one. My mind wanted to forget it. My body said no. Something was wrong; something had changed, seriously. When I saw my family physician, he went along with my mind's version, dismissing what had happened but ordering a cardiogram just to be sure. A week later he called to tell me it showed I had had a heart attack. He seemed uncertain of the medical details, but I hardly heard him; I was lost in a sense of sudden and profound change. In the moments of that call I became a different person.

surprised that he went to a party after the heart attack

During that week I had been asking, what's happening to me? My physician provided the medical answer, but it has taken me years to understand why it was not *my* answer. My physician was a model of politeness. We spoke over the phone as professionals: he called me Dr. Frank, I called him Dr. ———. We talked about my heart as if we were consulting about some computer that was producing errors in the output. "It" had a problem. Our talk was classier than most of the conversations I have with the mechanic who fixes my car, but only because my doctor and I were being vague. He was not as specific as my mechanic usually is. I knew more about hearts than I knew about cars, but this engine was inside me, so I was even more reluctant to hear about the scope of the damage.

What was wrong with that conversation, for me as an ill person, was precisely what made my physician's performance so professional. To be professional is to be cool and management oriented. Professional talk goes this way: A problem seems to have come up, more serious than we thought, but we can still manage it. Here's our plan; any questions? Hearing this talk, I knew full well that I was being offered a deal. If my response was equally cool and professional, I would have at least a junior place on the management team. I knew that as a patient's choices go, it wasn't a bad deal, so I took it. I was even vaguely complimented.

I did not yet know the cost of taking that deal. Experiences are to be lived, not managed. The body is not to be managed, even by myself. My body is the means and medium of my life; I live not only in my body but also through it. No one should be asked to detach his mind from his body and then talk about

True, doctors should not have to be emotional, but that's their job. If a doctor gets worked up over one patient, how is the doctor supposed to regain his composure in order to effectively treat the next patient?

this body as a thing, out there. No one should have to stay cool and professional while being told his or her body is breaking down, though medical patients always have to do just that. The demand being made of me was to treat the breakdown as if fear and frustration were not part of it, to act as if my life, the whole life, had not changed.

To others who have had or will have such a conversation, I must add that *I did not know what I wanted to say* or what I wanted the physician to say. I did not want to cry or scream or give a speech on the shortness of life. I'm not sure that what I wanted to say could be put into words. But I needed some recognition of what was happening to me. That day I became someone who had come very close to dying, and I might very soon come that close again. To become such a person is to change. After I heard that I had had a heart attack, how I lived in my body changed, and my doctor should have found a way to let me know he recognized that.

Being told I had had a heart attack required celebration. To celebrate is not necessarily to rejoice over an event but to mark its significance. A funeral celebrates a life. Tears and silence can celebrate an occasion just as kisses and handshakes do. But instead of my physician and I finding some terms to celebrate what was happening to me, we avoided recognizing the experience. We allowed ourselves to talk only about the mechanics of disease. I would have to learn to celebrate illness on my own.

The point is not that my physician was incompetent. On the contrary, he did exactly what professionals are trained to do. And I acted exactly as patients are trained to act. What is important for ill persons to understand is that there are limits to professional competence. Physicians too often do not express to the patient that they recognize her experiences of fear, frustration, and personal change. Their talk is about diseases, about the parts that have broken down, not about the whole, which is living that breakdown. But physicians' self-imposed limitations dictate the reciprocal roles patients are expected to play in responding to physicians. I was naive about physicians and illness and accepted these limitations. It thus took me much longer to recognize the power of illness to change my life and the way I think about myself.

The beginning of understanding was to recognize the difference between disease and illness. Medical talk uses disease terms that reduce the body to physiology, the organization of which can be measured. Disease terms include measures of body temperature, the presence or absence of infections, the circulation and composition of blood and other fluids, the texture of skin, and on and on. In disease talk these terms are used to indicate a breakdown, either present or imminent. Because the disease terms refer to measurements, they are "objective." Thus in disease talk *my* body, my ongoing experience of being alive, becomes *the* body, an object to be measured and thus objectified. "Objective" talk about disease is always medical talk. Patients quickly learn to express themselves in these terms, but in using medical expressions ill persons lose themselves: the body I experience cannot be reduced to the body someone else measures.

When a person becomes a patient and learns to talk disease talk, her body is spoken of as a place that is elsewhere, a "site" where the disease is happening. In speaking this way the patient identifies with the physician, for whom the patient's

Doctor does need to recognize fears, frustrations, etc. of the patient, but there should be a counselor there to help deal with the emotional aspects.

body *is* elsewhere. Since the ill person can see that it is far safer and more comfortable to be the physician, this confusion of identity is understandable, but it remains mistaken. The cost of this confusion to the ill person is forgetting that she exists as part of "it."

Illness is the experience of living through the disease. If disease talk measures the body, illness talk tells of the fear and frustration of being inside a body that is breaking down. Illness begins where medicine leaves off, where I recognize that what is happening to my body is not some set of measures. What happens to my body happens to my life. My life consists of temperature and circulation, but also of hopes and disappointments, joys and sorrows, none of which can be measured. In illness talk there is no such thing as *the* body, only *my* body as I experience it. Disease talk charts the progression of certain measures. Illness talk is a story about moving from a perfectly comfortable body to one that forces me to ask: What's happening to *me*? Not *it*, but *me*.

Medical treatment, whether in an office or hospital or on the phone, is designed to make everyone believe that only the disease — what is measurable and mechanical — can be discussed. Talking to doctors always makes me conscious of what I am *not* supposed to say. Thus I am particularly silent when I have been given bad news. I know I am supposed to ask only about the disease, but what I feel is the illness. The questions I want to ask about my life are not allowed, not speakable, not even thinkable. The gap between what I feel and what I feel allowed to say widens and deepens and swallows my voice.

Physicians are generally polite about answering questions,

[handwritten margin note: Again, save this for the Shrink]

but to ask a question one must already imagine the terms of an answer. My questions end up being phrased in disease terms, but what I really want to know is how to live with illness. The help I want is not a matter of answering questions but of witnessing attempts to live in certain ways. I do not want my questions answered; I want my experiences shared. But the stress and multiple demands on physicians and nurses too often push such sharing outside the boundaries of "professional" activity.

The more extreme the situation, the more time and help I need to say anything. When I face someone who does not seem willing or able to help me work toward what I might eventually say, I become mute. A person who finds no one willing to take the time and offer the help necessary to bring forth speech will protect himself by saying nothing. But the time when I cannot immediately put something into words is usually the time when I most need to express myself. Having no questions hardly means having nothing to say. You cannot be told that you have had a heart attack without having a great deal to express and needing to express it. The problem is finding someone who will help you work out the terms of that expression.

After five years of dealing with medical professionals in the context of critical illness, as opposed to the routine problems I had had before, I have accepted their limits, even if I have never become comfortable with them. Perhaps medicine should reform itself and learn to share illness talk with patients instead of imposing disease talk on them. Or perhaps physicians and nurses should simply do what they already do well — treat the breakdowns—and not claim to do more. This

Perhaps, nurses and physicians could present stories of others who have suffered in similar ways, or arrange meetings with others who have suffered. A type of volunteer program.

book will not resolve that question. What I offer ill persons is more immediate. Recognize that more is happening to you than you can discuss with most physicians in most medical settings. To talk about illness you must go elsewhere.

I have needed talk to express the changes that illness has brought to my life; through talk I continue to work out new ways of living with those changes. Critically ill persons need talk that recognizes all that they are experiencing. They need to talk not only for themselves, but also for those who are not yet ill. Illness can teach us all how to live a saner, healthier life. Illness is a threat to life, but it also witnesses what is worth living. However much suffering there is and however much we want to avoid being ill, we may need illness. Expressing that need, finding the terms in which to celebrate illness, is the task that lies head.

Illness as Incident

HEART PROBLEMS teach you how quickly life can go out of a body. My fear was that I would go to sleep and not wake up again. Having a heart attack is falling over the edge of a chasm and then being pulled back. Why I was pulled back made no more sense than why I fell in the first place. Afterward I felt always at risk of one false step, or heartbeat, plunging me over the side again. I will never lose that immanence of nothingness, the certainty of mortality. A heart attack is a moment of death. Once the body has known death, it never lives the same again.

People who think of themselves as healthy walk that edge too, but they see only the solid ground away from the chasm. Knowing that you walk on the edge is not just an experience of fear; it is also a clarification. I have hiked trails high in the Rocky Mountains, climbing through thick fog. At a certain altitude the fog clears, and suddenly I can see all that lies below me. It may be a long drop to the bottom, but the view is spectacular, and it is only at the moment of clearing that I know where I am.

I was not able to do much hiking in the period after my heart attack. Medicine's suspicion was that a viral infection had worked its way into my heart muscle. As a physician said to me, sometimes it's just a virus, sometimes you get myocarditis (an infection of the heart muscle), sometimes encephalitis (inflammation of the brain). When I heard this, my image of the path along the chasm's edge narrowed still further. I underwent a series of stress tests that monitored my heart while I ran on a treadmill. It was a relief to be running again, even in a hospital lab. The problem was that certain irregularities continued to show up in my heartbeat. My pulse rose much faster than it should have. My cardiologist could not rule out arterial blockage as the cause of my heart attack.

By September, six months after I had passed out, I felt better, but my stress tests were looking worse, and a decision was made to move on to the next diagnostic measure, an angiogram. This is a high-tech procedure in which a small incision is made near the groin and a catheter is passed through the vein into the heart. A dye is then injected into the heart through the catheter. The dispersion of the dye through the arteries is videotaped from X-ray monitors, and the cardiologist can locate any blockage. In addition, the rhythm of the heartbeat in the various chambers can be observed more closely than ultrasound procedures allow. The angiogram is done under local anesthetic, since the patient has to move around on command in order to get the proper X-ray angles.

The idea of having a catheter passed through a vein into my heart was mildly terrifying, though this part of the angiogram involved no sensation whatsoever. I had not looked forward to the procedure, but it was exciting. The injection of the dye produced a flush throughout my body that was almost pleasant enough to make up for the pinch of the initial incision. But the real excitement was on the television screen, where I watched my own heart beat and saw the dye spread out through the arteries.

At the time, however, I was less interested in seeing my heart than in knowing what the dispersion of the dye would show. Fortunately it showed a strong, regular heartbeat and no arterial blockage. For six months I had felt under a sentence of indeterminate doom. Hearing the cardiologist's immediate judgment of "good arteries" lifted that sentence. He went on to tell me that I could resume my normal athletic activities. I asked whether he would do any more stress tests, and he wisely replied no, he had a pretty good idea what they would show. Apparently running in hospital labs does not suit me; my heart wanted to get back outdoors. Outdoors I went, hardly looking back.

It would not be fair to myself to say I learned nothing from what happened. The next morning I had the thrill of remembering — as I remember it today — what my own heart looked like, beating on those television monitors. After months of staring at the abstract cardiograms of my heartbeat, here at last was a chance to see the real thing in action. Ours is the first age in history when people can look inside themselves and see their vital organs working. Even if that vision of inner space is mediated by a television screen, it is an adventure to behold. I had the sense to appreciate that.

Mostly, however, I wanted to escape from the world of illness and forget my view of the chasm. When I went for a final checkup several months later, my cardiologist told me I had been lucky that day in March; it could have ended differently. He also told me that if the virus recurred I would have a slightly increased immunity to it. Moreover, we now knew my arteries were in fine shape and, given my age, they would probably stay that way. I was more than willing to define what had happened as what medicine calls an "incident." It was a flat tire on the road of life, an annoying but minor breakdown. Some time had been lost, I had gotten a little dirty while repairs were made, but the tire was patched and I could continue the journey as if nothing had happened. It was only an incident, an interlude of no real consequence.

he was very lucky

Some time later I read a wonderful passage by Robert Louis Stevenson in which he described his youthful travel in southern France: "And I blessed God that I was free to wander, free to hope, and free to love." After my cardiologist told me to resume my life without restriction or fear, there were no boundaries on what I felt free to do. Being pronounced cured did not restore me to my previous physical condition; I could still run only a hundred yards without losing my breath. But I was free to try whatever I wanted. I was even free not to look back on what had happened.

Illness is a restriction. At best it requires spending time in treatment and enduring limitations on one's activity. At worst it deforms and impairs the body and cages the mind. Whenever I walk out of a hospital or a doctor's office, some part of me repeats the Stevenson quotation, and I too bless God for my freedom. But if freedom requires good health, it is precarious indeed. My heart attack should have taught me how little control we have over the condition of our bodies. My "incident" was, so far as anyone knows, the luck of the viral dice, and my recovery was no less a matter of chance, a contingency.

Thinking of my heart attack as an incident left me free to wander, but that freedom was based on an illusion that my health was unassailable. I had had my one breakdown, and now I was entitled to smooth traveling for the rest of the trip. All I thought of those who were not set free from illness, whose luck was not so good, was "Poor devils." By denying what I ought to have learned about my own vulnerability, I left myself more vulnerable still.

We are vulnerable creatures; that is what we share as humans. Being free to wander, hope, and love does not mean denying our vulnerability; rather it means embracing it. Only when we act in full knowledge of our vulnerability do we learn to discriminate. This does not mean simply choosing to wander here rather than there, hoping for this and not that, loving one rather than another. It means finding at the core of each activity an affirmation of living that goes beyond the particular choices of where, what, and whom.

When we wander, hope, and love as an affirmation of life rather than as a pursuit of this or that choice, we no longer depend on good health. When I left that cardiologist's office I had not had enough bad health to know how or why this is so. Within the year I would learn that the ill or impaired may, in the sense of fulfilling life, be far more free than healthy people. The healthy require health as an affirmation that their will is still effective, and they must continually prove this effectiveness. The ill accept their vulnerability as an affirmation that the world is perfect without any exercise of their will,

(margin handwritten notes:)

assuming that "It couldn't happen to me."

Take health for granted

Scary, but true

and this acceptance is their freedom. But to understand this I had to learn a different version of recovery, not from an incident but from an illness.

Defining my heart attack as an incident left me dependent on good health, which I once again assumed as my right. I still did not know how to enjoy health without making it a condition of my life. We are free only when we no longer require health, however much we may prefer it.

Becoming Ill Again

FIFTEEN MONTHS after my heart attack I was once again feeling healthy. In July I competed in a swim-bike-run triathlon, finished within a minute of my time two years earlier, and decided I was back where I had been. That was what I wanted from recovery — to get back to where I was before. But even in those terms, all was not well. When drying myself off after showering, I began to notice a persistent soreness in one testicle. Since childhood I have tended to have "swollen glands" as a response to viral infection, and at first I thought little of the soreness. As the discomfort increased I began to do what all men should do regularly: examine my testicles. I could feel a sharp ridge that had formed around the lower third of the left one. It felt as if the normal oval shape was turning into a figure eight, reminding me of the picture in my high school biology text of a cell about to divide. This was not what the testicle looked like but how it felt.

I suspected cancer because my "professional" training had given me the little bit of knowledge that, as the cliché correctly says, is a dangerous thing. When I was a graduate student in

makes me nervous

the early 1970s, I attended a seminar with a visiting sociologist whose specialty was epidemiology, the study of the distribution of diseases in geographical and social space. Social epidemiologists are particularly interested in how diseases vary by age, sex, race, and "social class" factors such as income, education, and type of employment. In the course of the seminar our visitor mentioned one of the most baffling diseases he had studied, cancer of the testes.

I had never heard of testicular cancer. While it came as no surprise that you could have cancer there, it was not what any man wants to hear. Most upsetting was the profile of those who get testicular cancer: young men, almost all white and predominantly in middle- and upper-middle-class jobs. It was, he joked, very much a disease of young university professors. No researcher understood why testicular cancer had this profile because nothing about the habits, risks, or lifestyle of this group seemed to suggest a connection. But there it was. The worst news was the prognosis. We were told that testicular cancer was one of the most lethal cancers, virtually untreatable, with a life expectancy of about six months. What dying was like was left to our imaginations.

There seems to be an increased risk of testicular cancer among men who had undescended testicles as a child, but beyond this we know nothing about the cause of the disease. However, the visiting professor was wrong, even then, in saying that testicular cancer was untreatable. Today it is one of the most successfully treated forms of cancer, though success varies, depending on how early it is diagnosed.

When I felt that ridge developing on my own testicle, I knew enough to think of cancer but not enough to realize it could be treated. What I remembered from that seminar sounded like a particularly unattractive death sentence, a painful and degrading way to go. Panicked but not totally irrational, I quickly made an appointment with my doctor. He looked somewhat distressed when I told him what was wrong, but he examined me, and to our mutual relief said he felt nothing that might be cancer. The left testicle felt smaller and harder, but nothing suggested a tumor. This was, of course, exactly what I wanted to hear. I was so relieved that I hardly thought to question his diagnosis of chlamydia, a disease that was new to me at that time.

Although easily cured in men, chlamydia is legally quarantinable because it is a leading cause of infertility in women. My doctor told me I might have gotten chlamydia from a public toilet or a hot tub, and did not tell me I had to take precautions against transmitting it sexually. He did not even ask me whether I was married or had sexual partners. Given his lack of advice and the danger chlamydia would have been to my wife, it is fortunate in one sense that his diagnosis was wrong.

Surprised the doctor didn't give more details concerning chlamydia

But on that day I was only too happy to accept his diagnosis. I could relax; I did not have cancer, and I was not aware of the problems associated with the chlamydia I thought I had. All I had to do was take some penicillin and everything would be fine. Why question a diagnosis that was so much better than the alternative? The answer, of course, is that my life was at stake — but I still retained my old belief that testicular cancer was a death sentence, so I clung to any alternative.

As the first prescription of penicillin ran out and the discomfort turned to pain, I had trouble sustaining my optimism. My doctor prescribed another course of penicillin, telling me

that these things take time to clear up. Soon after the testicle
soreness began, I had noticed an unfamiliar back pain while
running. I had attributed this to the muscular stress of getting
back into shape after my heart problems, but now the pain
was becoming intense, waking me in the morning. My physician confirmed the muscular nature of the back pain, de-
clared it unrelated to the testicular soreness, and switched my
drug prescription to sulfa, saying that sometimes penicillin
does not clear up chlamydia. When I had a reaction to the
sulfa, he took me off drugs entirely and made an appointment
for me to see a urologist — scheduled for two months later.

By early September my condition had deteriorated. The
back pains were so severe that I was forced to get up in the
middle of the night to relieve the pressure caused by lying on
my back. Rest was impossible. One Sunday morning after a
sleepless night I was in such pain that I could hardly stand.
Since I could expect little more from my usual physician, and
it was Sunday, Cathie drove me to the hospital emergency
room. When the routine blood and urine tests and X-ray
showed nothing abnormal, I was diagnosed as chronically
constipated and sent home with the advice to avoid dairy
products and eat more fruit. As I remember it, no "hands on"
examination was done; the lab tests were presumed to tell all.
At that point two physicians were telling me that nothing
much was wrong. I wanted to believe them, but my body
insisted otherwise.

To quiet my complaints about back pain, my physician sent
me to a sports medicine specialist. Nothing irritates me more
than politicians' and physicians' complaints about "doctor
shopping," or "double doctoring," as an equally insulting

phrase has it. If I had not doctor shopped for a *third* opinion, I would probably be dead, because the tumors involved in testicular cancer are among the fastest growing, and the success of treatment varies directly with early detection. Fortunately, the sports medicine specialist I saw was also a skilled internist. He had the good judgment to look beyond muscular-skeletal causes; he actually probed my abdomen with his hands, locating what felt like a mass. When I asked him what he thought this was, he mentioned the possibility of cancer. By then I felt less terrorized by the idea of cancer than validated by a recognition that I was seriously ill.

I had been in too much pain for too long, and I was relieved, at least momentarily, to be told that yes, he believed that something was wrong with me. Being told that you may have cancer does not have to be devastating. Even though my worst fears were realized in what he said, the physician showed, just by the way he looked at me and a couple of phrases he used, that he shared in the seriousness of my situation. The vitality of his support was as personal as it was professional. Physicians I encountered later were optimistic about my diagnosis and prognosis; he was almost alone in expressing optimism about me, not as a case but as a person.

With this third opinion on record, the medical investigation began to move. Several days later I was sent for an ultrasound, a noninvasive test often used for fetal monitoring. I seemed to be the only one in the waiting room who was not pregnant. Ultrasound is exciting for the patient because the physician can tell you what he is finding as he sees the X-ray images on a TV monitor next to you. In my case, however, the diagnosis was a little too exciting.

[handwritten margin note: amazed that other two doctors couldn't find the cancer]

Here I had half good luck — an excellent technician who was a terrible communicator. This physician told me he observed massive lymphadenopathy, or enlargement of the lymph nodes, behind my stomach. When I asked what would cause this, he abruptly told me it was either a primary or a secondary tumor. Either the nodes were malignant in themselves, or their growth was a development from a malignant tumor elsewhere. Looking back, I respect what that physician was able to discover. But at the time in that basement laboratory, all I could think about was being told I had massive tumors. The physician added nothing to his abrupt statement. He would send a report to my family physician; that was it, not even a goodbye or good luck, just over and out. It was a triumph of science and a lapse of humanity.

not very good bedside manner!

When I had left the sports medicine specialist's office I had felt that someone was taking my pain seriously and that a physician could be a source of real support. Walking out of the ultrasound lab, I faced the reality of cancer and felt completely alone. In the weeks before, I had been dealing with pain that made even walking difficult, but now that pain was only numbness.

What was it like to be told I had cancer? The future disappeared. Loved ones became faces I would never see again. I felt I was walking through a nightmare that was unreal but utterly real. This could not be happening to me, but it was, and it would continue to happen. My body had become a kind of quicksand, and I was sinking into myself, my disease.

Just as Cathie and I were putting our lives back together after my heart problems, cancer was ripping us up again, like the street near us that the city seems to dig up every year. As soon as it is paved and traffic is moving, some pipe breaks or some cable needs repair. Up go the roadblocks and in come the jackhammers. Our lives were like that: another year, another disaster.

After an incident like my heart attack I was able to bounce back. People even said, "You've really bounced back." That's accurate, because in most cases we do not sink into an experience, we only hit the surface. I may have bounced back from a heart attack, but with cancer I was going to have to sink all the way through and discover a life on the other side. Cancer was not going to be an incident; I would have to experience it.

Seeing Through Pain

HOW DOCTORS CAME to realize that I had cancer is only the institutional part of the story of becoming ill again. The medical experience has its place, but more important is what I was experiencing in my body. That story begins with pain. Medicine has not conquered pain, though it has developed the means to control pain during much of critical illness. Pain is experienced most at the beginning of illness, before physicians understand what is happening, and at the end, when the body becomes unpredictable. Since my experience happily did not reach that end, pain belongs at the beginning of my story.

Pain is the body's response to illness; it is the first thing many people associate with illness and what they fear most. Whether or not pain is the most difficult part of cancer to live through, it is probably the hardest to describe. We have plenty of words to describe specific pains: sharp, throbbing, piercing, burning, even dull. But these words do not describe the experience of pain. We lack terms to express what it means to live "in" such pain. Unable to express pain, we come to believe there is nothing to say. Silenced, we become isolated in pain, and the isolation increases the pain. Like the sick feeling that comes with the recognition of yourself as ill, there is a pain attached to being in pain.

My pain was the result of pressure exerted by the secondary tumors in my back, a pressure that became more acute when I lay down for some time. In the mornings I would wake up feeling a viselike pressure on my lower back around the kidneys. Soon the pain began to wake me at night, preventing me from sleeping. After several nights I was too tired to shake off sleep entirely, even though rest was impossible. I spent those nights in a kind of limbo between waking and dozing, always inside the pain.

My disease connected pain with night. As the tumors took over my body, pain took over my mind. Darkness compounds the isolation and loneliness of pain, for the sufferers are separated from those whose bodies lie quiet. In darkness the world of those in pain becomes unglued, incoherent.

In writing about the incoherence of pain, one risks becoming incoherent all over again. Language easily goes wrong. I could write that at night in pain I came to know illness face to face. But this metaphor distorts the experience. However much I wanted to give illness a face — to give it any kind of coherence — it is not a presence. Giving illness a face, a temptation enhanced by the dark, only muddles things further. At night I faced only myself.

When we feel ourselves being taken over by something we do not understand, the human response is to create a mythology of what threatens us. We turn pain into "it," a god, an enemy to be fought. We think pain is victimizing us, either because "it" is malevolent or because we have done something to deserve its wrath. We curse it and pray for mercy from it. But pain has no face because it is not alien. It is from myself. Pain is my body signaling that something is wrong. It is the body talking to itself, not the rumblings of an external god. Dealing with pain is not war with something outside the body; it is the body coming back to itself.

But taking pain entirely into my own body, making it too much my own, carries the danger of becoming isolated in that body. Isolation is the beginning of incoherence. When the body is healthy, it coheres, its parts work in concert, and it fits into its environment. Lying down, the body finds comfort and rest. Waking, it is ready for activity. In pain the natural rhythm of rest and activity is lost, and that loss leads to further losses of plans and expectations, of a life that makes sense as a fitting together of past and future. Order breaks down, and incoherence takes its place.

At night, while others are sleeping, it is coherent to sleep, to share that rest. To be summoned out of that rest is an incoherence, a loss of the wholeness that is the natural cycle of life among others. But again my language slips. No thing summoned me from sleep. Bodily pain woke me, and the consciousness of this pain turned into the incoherence of being awake, isolated from those who slept.

Pain is thus one of the first experiences an ill person has of being cast out. To regain a sense of coherence, in which pain may have to remain a part, the ill person has to find a way back in among those he has become separated from.

When I was awake at night in pain, I could have woken

Cathie. I could have called her to witness the pain and to break the loneliness, but waking her would have violated the coherence of her natural cycle of daily life. She still worked during the day and slept at night. Her life retained the coherence mine had lost. I was outside that natural cycle. During the day I was too tired to work, during the night the hammering in my back prevented me from sleeping. I was neither daily nor nocturnal, but suspended outside the limits of either existence. I was neither functionally present nor accountably absent. I lived my life out of place.

I used to have nightmares of finding myself in a place I knew to be forbidden, without any clothes and having to get back (in dreams you never know where) without being seen. Sometimes the nightmare would become an adventure. I would half fly and half flow, silent and naked, through dark, empty alleyways. Other times I would be caught out, fumbling and immobile, for all to see. Part of the fear in such dreams is of being out of place. I was no less out of place on those nights I half sat and half lay, trying to find a position outside of the pain.

I fantasized that this pain was "just for tonight," that it was muscular stress and would be gone tomorrow. This fantasy was fueled by my fear of what might truly be wrong with me, but it was also supported by what my doctor was telling me. One night he prescribed a strong sedative, and when I awoke even from that, the nightmares that accompanied me out of sleep did give incoherence a form and a face. After that night I could no longer sustain my part of what had been my doctor's and my mutual fantasy.

But I have only half-answered the question of why I did not

[margin note: Kind of an odd dream. Never had one of these before.]

[margin note: Easy to think when you're suffering]

wake my wife. The other reason is that her sleep was the only coherence left. Although I could no longer share in others' rest, I cared for it all the more. If I could not sleep, I could still love her sleep. Disturbing it would have been the most painful thing I could do. Later, when I was very ill, I watched people out running and loved their capacity for movement, their freedom within their bodies. My hope was that they also valued what they were able to be.

[handwritten margin note: reminds me of when I had bad insomnia, I valued sleep, even if it wasn't me that was sleeping]

I wish I could finish my story about pain with some formula I learned for dealing with it. But I never learned one. By the time I entered the hospital, the tumors had shifted or somehow changed, allowing me to lie in bed comfortably. There is probably some medical explanation for this change, but it does not interest me much. What counts is that the pain did its proper work: it forced me to get another medical opinion. By the date of the urology appointment made by my family physician, I had already had surgery and one chemotherapy treatment. Pain was the ally it is designed to be, my body's way of insisting that something must change.

Although I never discovered a formula for dealing with pain, I did manage to break through its incoherence one night before it abated. Making my way upstairs, I was stopped on the landing by the sight — the vision really — of a window. Outside the window I saw a tree, and the streetlight just beyond was casting the tree's reflection on the frosted glass. Here suddenly was beauty, found in the middle of a night that seemed to be only darkness and pain. Where we see the face of beauty, we are in our proper place, and all becomes coherent. As I looked at the window it formed a kind of haiku for me:

The streetlight behind the branches
Projects patterns
On a misted window
Do not wipe the glass
Lest others wake.

I realized that if illness has a face, it could be the beauty of
that light. But I did not see the face of illness in that window
any more than I had seen it in the nightmares caused by pain
breaking through the sedative. The window was no myth, no
metaphor. It was exactly what it was, and seeing it completely
absorbed my attention. I was still in pain, but the pain had
brought me to that landing, which was the only place I could
be to see the beauty of that window. Coherence was restored.

But coherence does not go without saying; it requires expression. However poor my verse was, I was once again expressing myself. Pain that is inexpressible isolates us; to be
mute is to be cast out from others. Whatever form our expression takes, we offer that expression to others, whether or
not anyone else is there. Expression implies the presence of
others, and we begin again to share in humanity. Others slept
their orderly sleep, and I, in my place as they were in theirs,
saw something of beauty. I remained alone, but my words put
me in the presence of those others.

It is just as hard to write about the coherence I felt as it is
to write about incoherence. But it does not matter if my words
are not coherent. For the ill person, the attempt to commu-
nicate creates an experience of coherence. The particular
words in my verse did not matter; it was my attempt at
expression that created coherence. I needed the window to see

the verse, and I needed the verse to place my seeing in the world of others and thus regain my place in that world.

It is easier to write of caring. I knew that others were sleeping, and I cared for their sleep; I knew there were things of beauty in the night that I cared for. These feelings made pain something I could live with. At the moment when the incoherence of illness and pain makes it seem that all you have lived for has been taken away or is about to be lost, you can find another coherence in which to live. That night the pain mattered less, not because I dissociated myself from my body, but rather because I associated myself beyond my body. Caring for Cathie's sleep or for that window gave me the coherence I needed to go on caring for myself. I had not yet been sick enough to understand all I saw in that window; only later would language catch up to experience. But at least that night I knew I was in a place I could care for.

Mourning What Is Lost

THE LOSS THAT accompanies illness begins in the body, as pain does, then moves out until it affects the relationships connecting that body with others. Those relationships first became strained during the weeks when I was getting bad medical news, but a diagnosis of cancer had not yet been confirmed. My body had lost its predictable capacity to sleep or walk, taking away my ability to make plans and accept responsibilities. But I did not want to believe I had cancer, and others did not want to hear about that possibility. My awkward attempts to avoid commitments I was not sure I could fulfill only made people think I was distancing myself from them. I acted not from lack of friendship but because my body was taking me out of their natural flow of plans and expectations. Others took planning for granted; my future was pervaded by uncertainty. I lost my sense of belonging.

The inability to make specific plans is only the beginning of the loss of belonging. On the day the ultrasound tests showed lymphadenopathy, I made it home in pretty good control of myself. I was alone because my mother-in-law was beginning a new round of chemotherapy that day. Cathie and I had decided, perhaps in a moment of mutual denial of what was happening to me, that she should be with her mother. When I walked back into our house, she was still out, and what had happened crashed down on me. All I could see were faces I would never grow old with — my daughter from my first marriage, Cathie, my parents. I believed I was going to die, much sooner than later. The pain of my death was in losing my future with those others. My reasons for living have never been clearer.

Loss of the future is complemented by loss of the past. I felt this loss most keenly one night shortly before the surgery to remove the tumorous testicle. The surgery is called an orchidectomy or sometimes orchiectomy, from the Greek *orchi,* for testis. The name still reminds me of an exotic flower, which the operation would pluck. I found this amusing. The coming operation did not distress me; I had had too much pain to feel any great attachment to that part of my body. I was told I would have no impairment of sexual functioning from the loss of one testicle. If I had been in my late teens, as some testicular cancer patients are, the operation would have had a different meaning. At my age I was more interested in being able to pull on a pair of pants without wincing.

I did feel I was losing my body's continuity with its youth. Middle age insinuates itself slowly into our bodies and lives. It is the time when on a good day you can still kid yourself into thinking you are as young as ever. Several nights before surgery, I looked at myself in a mirror. The body I saw was not the body I had had at twenty-two or even thirty, but it retained for me a continuity with those bodies. The changes, the deteriorations, had been gradual. On another night I might have been able to kid myself into seeing the thirty-year-old.

That night I knew that after surgery I would never be the same. By then I was aware that chemotherapy could effectively shrink the tumors along my back. Even so, I would not be the same. Surgery and chemotherapy would irrevocably break my body's continuity with its past. I did not dread what I would become, but I needed to mourn the end of what I had been. It was like saying goodbye to a place I had lived in and loved. I had tried to take care of my body, and it had treated me well enough, but now treatments I did not yet understand would change it into something else.

When you say goodbye to your body, as I was doing that night, you say goodbye to how you have lived. An old aphorism says that after a certain age every man is responsible for his own face. Each person records the history of his life on his body. My history had it share of regrets, but I mourned its passing. After surgery and chemotherapy rearranged me, I would live differently. This difference is made up of gains as much as losses, but at that moment the gains were unknowable and the losses were before me in the mirror.

Other losses went beyond the body. Cathie and I had always hoped that if the worst happened, friends and relatives would respond with care and involvement. Then the worst did happen, and we no longer expected what others would do, we knew. Some came through; others disappeared. We now find it hard to resume relationships with those who could not acknowledge the illness that was happening, not just to me but to us. Those relationships were a loss.

Together Cathie and I lost an innocence about the normal expectations of life. At one time it seemed normal to expect to work and accomplish certain things, to have children and watch them grow, to share experiences with others, to grow old together. Now we realize that these events may or may not happen. Life is contingent. We are no longer sure what it is normal to expect. At a later time this loss of innocent expectation can be seen as a gain from illness, but at first it feels like a loss.

These losses of future and past, of place and innocence, whether they are ours together or mine alone, must all be mourned. The ill person's losses vary according to one's life and illness. We should never question what a person chooses to mourn. One person's losses may seem eccentric to another, but the loss is real enough, and that reality deserves to be honored. I was fortunate to have a wife to share my mourning. Sharing losses seemed to be the gentlest way of living with them.

I have written of my own losses and something of ours together, but nothing of the losses that were Cathie's alone. Even now I probably recognize only some of these. The caregiver often has more difficulty finding time and recognition for mourning. While I was ill we knew that she, the caregiver, needed to mourn and recognize losses as much as I, the ill person. We both had to let our grieving run its course. But despite our intentions, this natural sequence did not happen. Before we had time to mourn the experience of my illness, Cathie's mother became critically ill and eventually died. During her illness the levels of mourning were compounded, and we had to place our earlier mourning on hold. Through these experiences we learned how the failure to mourn impairs a life.

Most people's problems with mourning are not caused by compounded losses; their problems are caused by other people's desires to get mourning over with. Medical staff, family, and friends all want the ill person or caregiver to accommodate to loss, whether it is caused by illness or by death, as quickly as possible. Mourning slows down the treatment of the ill and reminds others of their own mortality. Society pressures us to return to the healthy mainstream, minimizing and forgetting our losses.

Professionals talk too much about adjustment. I want to emphasize mourning as affirmation. To mourn what has passed, either through illness or death, affirms the life that has been led. To adjust too rapidly is to treat the loss as simply an incident from which one can bounce back; it devalues whom or what has been lost. When an ill person loses the body in which she has lived, or when a caregiver suffers the death of the person he has cared for, the loss must be mourned fully and in its own time. Only through that mourning can we find a life on the other side of loss.

I suggested that this book is in some sense a series of letters to my younger self before I became ill. I want to tell that self to let yourself grieve your losses and to find people who will accept that grieving. Avoid those who seek to minimize what you have lost, whether by comparing your losses to those of others or by telling you you'll soon get used to it. The losses you go through are real, and no one should take these away from you. They are a part of your experience, and you are entitled to them. Illness can teach that every part of life is worth experiencing, even the losses. To grieve well is to value what you have lost. When you value even the feeling of loss, you value life itself, and you begin to live again.

adjust, but not too rapidly
if you dwell on something for too long, it can
tear you up inside and possibly led to depression
don't deny death, accept it, then move on
it will make you stronger

Care Has No Recipe

THE ORDER of the previous chapters may suggest that the experience of illness follows a sequence: first pain, then loss, and so on. Writing creates an illusion of order, but in life experiences overlap. More important, what happened to me was mine alone. The value of telling one particular story in detail is that it shows how unique each of us is. I do not want to generalize my experience of illness into some set of stages. Only by recognizing the differences in our experiences can we begin to care for each other.

My experiences with heart attack and cancer taught me how different illnesses can be. The first difference is in our fears. With heart problems my fears were of sudden disappearance. But at least as I imagined it, I would have gone out like the athlete dying young in the poem of that title. In full flower, as I thought of it. Thirty-nine is not that young, and I was never much of an athlete, but in imagining my own death I allowed myself some poetic license.

With most cancers there is little fear of sudden death. When I went to sleep I was sure I would wake up in the morning. The problem with cancer is, wake up to what? My fear was less of being dead than of dying slowly, of decaying, suffering interminably, the body spewing out foul fluids. I have now been yuck with enough people dying of cancer to know that their deaths involve fewer of the gruesome details than I feared. Popular fears of cancer, which I shared, exaggerate the drama of its terrors but underestimate the mundane discomforts that accumulate. If a heart attack blows you away, cancer chips at you bit by bit.

Fears vary. Differences in fears are part of the individual experience of illness, and care is about recognizing difference. Care must also recognize how differently people may experience the same disease. How people learn that they have cancer makes a lasting difference. I discovered cancer through pain. One day, before I was diagnosed, I was trying to walk from our home to the university where I teach. It's an easy walk, and I enjoy it. Walking clears my mind. But this day I felt like a balloon was being blown up inside my rib cage, constricting me. I was suffocating from within; stopping did not relieve the pressure. As I got to campus I passed a colleague and found I could not speak to him. I just could not make any words form.

Having that experience prepared me for the medical diagnosis and treatment that came later. Before I called it cancer, I already knew how serious the condition of my body was. I never want to repeat that suffocating, painful experience, but I appreciate having had it. The pain made what was happening to my body real. Other people are told that they have cancer before they have experienced it in their bodies. They find it difficult to know cancer as more than an abstraction.

Six years after her initial diagnosis of cancer, my mother-in-law remarked that she had never suffered from cancer itself. She suffered from medical interventions, but the success of these treatments prevented her from being aware of the disease's effect on her body. Once she bent over to pick up a pencil and felt a sharp pain from compression. She was both frightened and excited when her doctor told her she might have felt the tumors. It was the first time she actually experienced the disease they were treating. I am grateful she did not suffer more, but I think that for her cancer was mostly an abstraction. Cancer was something physicians talked about, and treatment was something they did to her. I think her illness was made more difficult by not having a sense of the disease in her body until near the end, but I doubt that one person can judge another's experience. I claim only that we came to know our illnesses in very different ways.

Another friend remembered the indignation she felt when a physician told her that "cancer was coursing through her body." His comment was devastating to her, but at times I would have found it validating. Whatever was happening in her body, what she was feeling was a tiny lump in her breast. My body was telling me that something awful *was* coursing through it — not a bad description. When I was hardly able to walk, but my family doctor was telling me simply to quit running and see a urologist in a couple of months, it was reassuring to have other physicians acknowledge that the problems were as real as I felt they were.

When I was finally told how sick I was, the essential difference between the diagnoses by the sports medicine specialist and the ultrasound physician was in the support each gave me. The two diagnoses were about the same, but the sports medicine physician involved himself in what he was telling me, while the other physician pronounced his diagnosis like a verdict. Differences proliferate: the same message can have different meanings for different ill persons, and the same content can become two different messages, depending on how it is delivered.

Care begins when difference is recognized. There is no "right thing to say to a cancer patient," because the "cancer patient" as a generic entity does not exist. There are only persons who are different to start with, having different experiences according to the contingencies of their diseases. The common diagnostic categories into which medicine places its patients are relevant to disease, not to illness. They are useful for treatment, but they only get in the way of care.

Most people who deal with ill persons do not want to recognize differences and particularities because sorting them out requires time. Even to learn what the differences are, you have to become involved. Generalities save time. Placing people in categories, the fewer the better, is efficient; each category indicates a common treatment: one size fits all. But again, treatment is not care. Treatment gets away with making a compromise between efficiency and care by creating an illusion of involvement. This illusion often begins with a recipe, made up of key words referring to psychological states, that tells treatment providers what behavior to expect.

The most famous recipe is Elisabeth Kübler-Ross's stage theory of the experience of dying: the dying person goes through denial, anger, bargaining, grief, and acceptance. Although I do not think it was Kübler-Ross's original intent, her theory has been used to categorize rather than to open up people's experiences. Instead of guiding us into what is particular about an individual's experiences with illness, these words create distance, allowing others to say, "As we expected, he's going through anger." Rather than asking why the ill person is angry, anger becomes "just a stage." And since we expected it, we can dismiss it as "something everyone goes through."

hard to change what we've been taught to do in certain situations

What makes an experience real is its particulars. One person's anger or grief may differ so much from another's that calling them by a common name only obscures what is actually going on for each. The word — anger, grief, or whatever — conceals more than it reveals. The popularity of such a theory is not surprising. Persons using such words think they can understand without having to become involved in the texture of lived experience with all its variations. They can even draw others into this illusion of understanding.

Stage theories can be valuable for ill persons, however, if not for caregivers. Those who are ill find it valuable to know that others share their experiences. When I was panicked by the diagnosis of cancer, I took comfort from knowing that panic is a "normal" reaction upon hearing a diagnosis of life-threatening disease. When I felt disoriented and depressed, I knew I wasn't going crazy; this too is normal. Knowing that others go through these experiences made my own panic, disorientation, and depression feel less personal, less specific to me. But the caregiver must remember that my panic *is* mine entirely, not some "stage." The last thing an ill person needs is to be treated as "only going through the panic stage." The individual's panic may be mitigated because it is shared, but it cannot be dismissed because it is expected.

makes you feel a little better; let's you know that others have felt the same

Knowing that panic is normal does not resolve the feelings evoked in that panic.

After persons receive a diagnosis of serious illness, the support they need varies as widely as humanity itself. Some want to have family gathered around them, others need to be alone. Some need the assurance of immediate medical intervention, others have to have some time to decide what treatment they want. A physician may help one person by rushing in, another, by backing off. The caregiver's art is finding a way to allow the ill person to express his needs. Eventually a balance must be worked out between what the ill person needs and what the caregivers are able to provide. In order to find that balance, caregivers, whether professional, family, or friends, must help the ill person figure out what he needs. Only then can they negotiate what they are prepared to provide.

It takes time for an ill person to understand her needs. The caregiver cannot simply ask "What do you need?" and expect a coherent reply. A recently diagnosed person's life has already changed in more ways than she can grasp, and changes continue throughout critical illness. Part of what is "critical" is the persistence of change. Being critically ill means never being able to keep up with your own needs. Except for the need to hear that it is all a mistake — the lab results had the wrong name on them; I'm fine, really — the ill person does not know what she needs, though the needs are very real.

The day I had the ultrasound, which strongly suggested that I had cancer, a visiting professor happened to be in town to act as external examiner for a Ph.D. candidate in my department. Cathie and I were supposed to take him to dinner that night. After the ultrasound she and I had some time to go through various emotions together. We acknowledged that what we each had feared was now real, we cursed the medical system for being so slow, and we tried to be optimistic about the physician I was now being sent to. We found ways to let each other know that our love carried on. Then we picked up our guest and went to dinner, with no mention of cancer.

His company was the perfect vehicle for the denial we needed that night. Being out with him put cancer on hold for awhile, and during that time we realized that there could still be pleasant evenings; life would go on, even with cancer. We could never have planned what happened, but we were able to use it to meet our needs. Perhaps you should not even try to put your needs into words. All you can do is let yourself discover these needs, and all others can do is give you the time and space to make this discovery.

I reserve the name "caregivers" for the people who are willing to listen to ill persons and to respond to their individual experiences. Caring has nothing to do with categories; it shows the person that her life is valued because it recognizes what makes her experience particular. One person has no right to categorize another, but we do have the privilege of coming to understand how each of us is unique. When the caregiver communicates to the ill person that she cares about that uniqueness, she makes the person's life meaningful. And as that person's life story becomes part of her own, the caregiver's life is made meaningful as well. Care is inseparable from understanding, and like understanding, it must be symmetrical. Listening to another, we hear ourselves. Caring for another, we either care for ourselves as well, or we end in burnout and frustration.

Most medical staff do not have the time to be caregivers, and many may not have the inclination. They provide treatment, which is no less important than caregiving, but it is not at all the same. Too often even the family members who remain involved with the ill person rather than defecting also become service providers rather than caregivers. *— don't know any better trying their best*

Caregivers are confronted not with an ordered sequence of illness experiences, but with a stew of panic, uncertainty, fear, denial, and disorientation, with bargaining quickly added. Cathie had to listen for days to my bargaining one diagnostic or treatment possibility against another. "I'll suffer this if I don't have to have that." It takes the ill person some time to realize there is nothing and no one to bargain with. Loneliness also enters, then doubts about who you are and what your life is worth, hope mixed with depression, anger mixed with a desire for contact with others, dependency mixed with a need to continue to do things for yourself.

What I have just written only suggests the stew of an ill person's feelings, but even that returns me to my central point: none of these words mean anything. Terms like pain or loss have no reality until they are filled in with an ill person's own experience. Witnessing the particulars of that experience, and recognizing all its differences, is care.

The Body as Territory
and as Wonder

HAVE PUT my body in the hands of physicians off and on since the day I was born. But until I was critically ill I never felt I was putting my life in their hands. Life-threatening illness gave doctors a new dimension of importance for me. I had never expected so much from them or been so sensitive to their shortcomings. How medicine treats the body is an essential part of the story of illness, but it is never more than half of the story. The other half is the body itself. Life-threatening illness also gave my body a new dimension of importance. I had never been so sensitive to its shortcomings, nor had I realized how much I could expect of it. These two stories, the story of medicine taking the body as its territory and the story of learning to wonder at the body itself, can only be told together, because illness is both stories at once.

After the ultrasound a physician said, "This will have to be investigated." Hearing this phrase, I was both relieved and offended. The relief was that someone was assuming part of the burden of worrying about what was happening to me. But

I was also offended by his language, which made my body into medicine's field of investigation. "I" had become medicine's "this." The physician did not even say, "We'll have to find out what's wrong with you," which would have been a team of real people ("we") speaking to another person ("you"). "This will have to be investigated" was not addressed to me at all. The physician was speaking as if to himself, allowing me, the patient, to overhear.

"This will have to be investigated" assumes that physicians will do the investigation, but they too are left out of the phrase, anonymous. "Will have to be" suggests the investigation happens of its own necessity. Why should a physician speak this way? Because if in the course of this investigation mistakes are made (as the physician who spoke had already mistaken my diagnosis), no individual physician is responsible. The mistakes are just part of a process; they too "have to be." I imagine he spoke out of fear as well as uncertainty. He responded by making himself and other physicians anonymous. And I had to be made equally anonymous.

I, my body, became the passive object of this necessity, the investigation. I could imagine how native people felt when European explorers arrived on their shores, planted a flag, and claimed their land on behalf of a foreign monarch who would bring civilization to the savages. To get medicine's help, I had to cede the territory of my body to the investigation of doctors who were as yet anonymous. I had to be colonized.

The investigation required me to enter the hospital. Fluids were extracted, specialists' opinions accumulated, machines produced images of the insides of my body, but the diagnosis remained uncertain. One day I returned to my room and found a new sign below my name on the door. It said "Lymphoma," a form of cancer I was suspected of having. No one had told me that this diagnosis, which later proved to be wrong, had been confirmed. Finding it written there was like the joke about the guy who learns he has been fired when he finds someone else's name on his office door. In this case my name had not been changed, it had been defined. "Lymphoma" was a medical flag, planted as a claim on the territory of my body.

This colonization only became worse. During chemotherapy a nurse, speaking to Cathie, referred to me as "the seminoma in 53" (my room number). By then the diagnosis was correct, but it had crowded out my name entirely. The hospital had created its own version of my identity. I became the disease, the passive object of investigation and later of treatment. Nameless, how could I be a person who experiences?

The ill person actively tries to make sense of what is happening in her body. She tries to maintain a relationship between what is happening to her body and what is going on in the rest of her life. When a person becomes a patient, physicians take over her body, and their understanding of the body separates it from the rest of her life. Medicine's understanding of pain, for instance, has little to do with the ill person's experience. For the person, pain is about incoherence and the disruption of relations with other people and things; it is about losing one sense of place and finding another. Medicine has no interest in what pain means in a life; it can see pain only as a symptom of a possible disease. Medicine cannot enter into the experience; it seeks only cure or management. It does offer relief to a body that is suffering, but in doing so it colonizes the body. This is the trade-off we make in seeking medical help.

If the treatment works, the passivity is worth it. When I am ill, I want to become a patient. It is dangerous to avoid doctors, but it is equally dangerous to allow them to hog center stage in the drama of illness. The danger of avoiding doctors is immediate and physical, but if we allow them to dominate the drama, they will script it to include only disease. By saying "This will have to be investigated," my physician claimed center stage and scripted the drama to follow; the person within my body was sent out into the audience to watch passively.

What did I, as patient, want from physicians and the medical staff? I did not expect to become friends with them. In the hospital I had such fleeting contact with so many specialists, and nurses appeared to rotate through shifts so rapidly, that exchanging anything more than conventional pleasantries would have been artificial. The relationship of patient to staff is peculiar, unlike any other. We discussed intimate matters, but this talk did not make us close. As treatment providers, they saw my intimate concerns in the context of their general categories of disease and the progress of treatment.

Relationships between patients and medical staff, whether physicians or nurses, involve people who are intimate with each other but rarely become intimates of each other. For a truly intimate relationship people need a sharing of time and personal history and a recognition of each other's differences. Medical intimacy categorizes rather than recognizes, and it is one-sided. The patient's life and body are an open book, or chart, to the medical staff. The staff sometimes share their experiences with patients, but in my memory these moments are the exceptions. More important, physicians and nurses can choose what they will tell a patient about themselves, and whether they will say anything at all. There is the real asymmetry, which becomes more complicated during moments that are critical in the patient's life but represent just another day's work for the staff. The staff cannot match the patient's emotional intensity on such occasions, but they should not expect the patient to mimic their professional calm.

I may not expect emotion or intimacy from physicians and nurses, but I do expect recognition. Another person, whose experience I want to honor, said it is no small thing to have cancer — to realize you are becoming ill, to suffer that illness and risk death, to be dying or to have returned to the living and be starting life over again with the knowledge of your own mortality. It is no small thing to have your body rearranged, first by disease and then by surgical and chemical interventions intended to cure that disease. Critical illness takes its travelers to the margins of human experience. One step further and someone so ill would not return. I want that journey to be recognized.

I always assumed that if I became seriously ill, physicians, no matter how overworked, would somehow recognize what I was living through. I did not know what form this recognition would take, but I assumed it would happen. What I experienced was the opposite. The more critical my diagnosis became, the more reluctant physicians were to talk to me. I had trouble getting them to make eye contact; most came only to see my disease. This "it" within the body was their field of investigation; "I" seemed to exist beyond the horizon of their interest.

Medical staff often believe they are involved in the patient's personal life. When I was admitted to the hospital, the resident doing my intake physical made a point of saying he was now getting to the "social history." Cathie and I were curious to know what the hospital considered important as social history. The resident then asked what my job was. I answered and waited for the next question; he closed the chart. That was it, nothing more. What bothered us was the illusion that he had found out something. The resident took his inquiry into my social history seriously and seemed to have no sense of how little he learned. The irony of there being only one question completely escaped him. He was filling in a category, employment, to give himself an illusion of having recognized me as a "social" being.

[margin note: that's interesting, kind of odd to ask just one "social history" question and no more]

The night before I had surgery, I was visited by an anesthesiologist who represented the culmination of my annoyance with this nonrecognition. He refused to look at me, and he even had the facts of the planned operation wrong. When he was leaving I did the worst thing to him I could think of: I made him shake hands. A hand held out to be shaken cannot be refused without direct insult, but to shake a hand is to acknowledge the other as an equal. The anesthesiologist trembled visibly as he brushed his hand over mine, and I allowed myself to enjoy his discomfort. But that was only a token of what I really wanted. I wanted him to recognize that the operation I was having and the disease it was part of were no small thing.

[margin note: anesth. seems really rude]

The kind of recognition I wanted changed over the course of my illness. While seeking diagnosis I felt that I was in a struggle just to get physicians to recognize the disease; once I got them onto the stage of my illness, the problem was to keep it my drama, not theirs. The active roles in the drama of illness all go to physicians. Being a patient means, quite literally, being patient. Daily life in the hospital is spent waiting for physicians. Hospitals are organized so that physicians can see a maximum number of patients, which means patients spend maximum time waiting. You have to be patient. Maybe the doctor will come this morning; if not, maybe this afternoon. Decisions about treatment are stalled until the doctor's arrival; nurses and residents don't know what's happening. Hopes, fears, and uncertainty mount.

Seems like you wait forever I hate that!,

When the physician does arrive, he commands center stage. I write "he" because this performance is so stereotypically masculine, although women physicians learn to play it well enough. The patient hangs on what brief words are said, what parts of the body are examined or left unattended. When the physician has gone, the patient recounts to visitors everything he did and said, and together they repeatedly consider and interpret his visit. The patient wonders what the physician meant by this joke or that frown. In hospitals, where the patient is constantly reminded of how little he knows, the physician is assumed not only to know all but to know more than he says.

In becoming a patient — being colonized as medical territory and becoming a spectator to your own drama — you lose yourself. First you may find that the lab results rather than your body's responses are determining how you feel. Then, in the rush to treatment, you may lose your capacity to make choices, to decide how you want your body to be used. Finally, in the blandness of the medical setting, in its routines and their discipline, you may forget your tastes and preferences. Life turns to beige. It is difficult to accept the realities of what physicians can do for you without subordinating yourself to their power. The power is real, but it need not be total. You can find places for yourself in the cracks.

I want to affirm the importance, both for yourself and for those around you, of holding onto the person you still are, even as medicine tries to colonize your body. Disease cannot be separated from other parts of a person's identity and life. Disease changed my life as husband, father, professor, and everything else. I had to learn to be dependent. I was unreliable in practical matters and often in emotional ones as well, and incapable of doing tasks that I had considered normal. It was no small thing to rediscover myself as I changed.

I have learned that the changes that begin during illness do not end when treatment stops. Life after critical illness does not go back to where it was before. A danger of allowing physicians to dominate the drama of illness is that they leave as soon as the disease is resolved to their satisfaction or when they have done all they can. Then the ill person and those around him are left to deal with the consequences of what has not been recognized. If the ill person dies, those who survive must deal with all that was not said, the unfinished business of a life closed out in a setting where dying is a problem of management, not a continuity of experience. And those ill persons who recover must recover not only from the disease but from being a patient. This recovery will proceed far more smoothly if the person within the patient has been recognized throughout the period of illness and recovery.

Continuing to recognize myself as the person undergoing

the illness, reclaiming my body as my territory while I was in settings dominated by what was relevant to medicine alone, was no easy business.

What authorizes medicine to claim the body as its territory? Every day society sends us messages that the body can and ought to be controlled. Advertisements for prescription and nonprescription drugs, grooming and beauty advice, diet books, and fitness promotion literature all presuppose an ideal of control of the body. Control is good manners as well as a moral duty; to lose control is to fail socially and morally. But then along comes illness, and the body goes out of control.

In society's view of disease, when the body goes out of control, the patient is treated as if he has lost control. Being sick thus carries more than a hint of moral failure; I felt that in being ill I was being vaguely irresponsible. Of course, the problem is not that I or any other ill person has "lost" control; the problem is that society's ideal of controlling the body is wrong in the first place. But rather than give up this ideal, society sends in physicians to prove that bodies can be controlled. Physicians justifiably think it is their duty to restore, in the name of society, the control that the sick are believed to have lost. Control, or at least management, becomes a medical ideal.

A cousin who had cancer wrote to me about a meeting she had with her doctor in which she asked more questions than he apparently thought appropriate. He accused her of "trying to control" her treatment, and asserted that he was "in control." This story is not uncommon, though it seems to happen more often to women patients than to men. The real question is not who is in control, but whether anyone is. One lesson I have learned from illness is that giving up the idea of control, by either myself or my doctors, made me more content. What I recommend, to both medical staff and ill persons, is to recognize the wonder of the body rather than try to control it.

Wondering at the body means trusting it and acknowledging its control. I do not mean that we should stop trying to change the direction the body is taking. I certainly did all I could, and I value all that my physicians did, to use treatment to change the direction my body was taking. Wonder and treatment can be complementary; wonder is an attitude in which treatment can best proceed. To think that any of us was controlling the body through treatment is another illusion. That my body responded to medical interventions did not mean it was being "successfully" controlled. Rather we should wonder at what "it" did. I use the word "it" here because the body worth wondering at is not the creature of my conscious mind. It is not an extension of "I." Instead, my mind is an extension of my body. I claim little credit for the wonder of my body.

Wonder is almost always possible; control may not be. If the ill person can focus on an ideal of wonder in place of control, then living in a diseased body can recover some of its joy. I did not think this up; I learned it from my body one morning in the rain.

While my investigation was still in the outpatient stage, I used to walk to the hospital for diagnostic tests. One morning I was scheduled to have a pyelogram, a kind of X-ray to test kidney functioning. Cathie was teaching and needed the car. It was pouring rain, coming down in buckets. Any sane person would have called a taxi, but I had cancer and no aspirations to sanity. I wanted to walk. Preparation for the pyelogram required taking massive laxatives to empty the intestine, so in addition to my sleeping problems, I had spent the night in the bathroom.

But as wrecked as I was, when I started walking I began to feel better. I was outside and moving and really very happy. First my feet began to get wet, then my pants, and soon the water was dripping inside my jacket, but that didn't matter. Here was the world of people going to work, of puddles and grass and leaves, and I was able to be part of it. Getting wet was the least of my problems. My problem was going into the hospital, or, more specifically, not coming out again. I feared that the pyelogram's results would mean I couldn't leave the hospital; soon the world I was walking through would be closed off to me. Not today probably; I half realized that before any results were available and medical judgment took over, I would have escaped. But I did not know how many more walks I might have. So I did not lapse into thinking about what I was going to do once I got where I was going; that day I experienced the trip. And I realized that I owed it to illness to be able to see that green September day so very clearly.

I did not want to arrive at the hospital, yet I knew I couldn't slosh around outside much longer. For the first time since the ultrasound several days before, I felt pleasantly relaxed about whatever was to happen. Going inside out of the rain, I wondered at what the body could still do for me, as diseased as I knew it must be. That day I stopped resenting "it" for the pain I had felt and began to appreciate my body, in some ways for the first time in my life. I stopped evaluating my body and began to draw strength from it. And I recognized that this body was me.

Later, when I was admitted to the hospital, the strange progress of my disease had relieved most of the pain, and I started exercising again. Exercising in a hospital is not easy. In Canadian hospitals one gets a private room only by the luck of the moment of arrival or by having some very infectious disease. I was lucky in my timing. I took advantage of my privacy to lift weights Cathie brought for me. Nurses would come in to record my vital signs and find I was out running up and down stairs. Their tolerance was more remarkable than my eccentricity.

Running on the stairs, experiencing the strength I still had, gave me a feeling that my body was doing what it wanted. Through exercise I began to discover what I wanted. Exercise was a way of keeping myself at center stage of my illness. When I had surgery, these activities had to end, but they got me through the period of finding "Lymphoma" written under my name. The hospital had its labels for me, but I could hold onto my identity, which was still rooted in my body, tumorous or not.

Exercising was also a way of telling myself that I would come back from cancer, that my body was still worth taking care of. This affirmation was not, however, a deal. I did not think exercise was part of any cure. It was the way I wanted to live out my life with illness, a way to keep living the life I had, regardless of the progress of disease. Exercise was my expression of wonder at the body.

The arts of being ill and of practicing medicine should

converge in mutual wonder at the body. A physician who does not have this sense of wonder seeks only to cure diseases. Sometimes he succeeds, but if cure is the only objective, not achieving it means he has failed. For the artful physician, wonder precludes failure. The physician and the ill person enter into a relationship of joint wonder at the body, in which failure is as irrelevant as control. The ill person who finds a physician to join in this wonder is fortunate. The body is not a territory to be controlled by either the physician's treatment or the patient's will. Those patients whose physicians remain rooted in disease and cure have to accept medical treatment for what it is, and learn to wonder alone or with other caregivers.

I hope that what I call wonder at the body will not be confused with the particular ways I used my body. It happened that I learned about my body by walking to the hospital and by exercising while I was a patient there, but these activities were not essential to continuing the process of wonder. After surgery I did not have many choices for using my body, and chemotherapy gave me even fewer, since by then I could not read. But I found other sources of coherence, particularly in music. At night when I put my head into a Walkman and listened to Bach, I could forget the implications of being in a hospital. Orchestral music was too busy when heard through my cheap headphones, but Glenn Gould playing the Goldberg Variations brought me a peace and identity my environment could not provide. Only later did I learn that Bach wrote the variations for an insomniac prince.

Listening to that music became an activity for my body. I love running most when moving is pervaded by a sense of rhythm, and listening to Bach's music gave me a sensation of movement. The origins of music are inseparable from dance, and dance is one of the great metaphors of life itself. Until I was ill I had never heard so clearly the dance in the music, and life in the dance. Illness taught me that beyond anything I can do, the body simply is. In the wisdom of my body's being I find myself, over and over again.

The Cost of Appearances

SOCIETY PRAISES ill persons with words such as *courageous, optimistic,* and *cheerful.* Family and friends speak approvingly of the patient who jokes or just smiles, making them, the visitors, feel good. Everyone around the ill person becomes committed to the idea that recovery is the only outcome worth thinking about. No matter what the actual odds, an attitude of "You're going to be fine" dominates the sickroom. Everyone works to sustain it. But how much work does the ill person have to do to make others feel good?

Two kinds of emotional work are involved in being ill. The kind I have written about in earlier chapters takes place when the ill person, alone or with true caregivers, works with the emotions of fear, frustration, and loss and tries to find some coherence about what it means to be ill. The other kind is the work the ill person does to keep up an appearance. This appearance is the expectation that a society of healthy friends, coworkers, medical staff, and others places on an ill person.

The appearance most praised is "I'd hardly have known she was sick." At home the ill person must appear to be engaged in normal family routines; in the hospital she should appear to be just resting. When the ill person can no longer conceal the effects of illness, she is expected to convince others that being ill isn't that bad. The minimal acceptable behavior is praised, faintly, as "stoical." But the ill person may not feel like acting good-humored and positive; much of the time it takes hard work to hold this appearance in place.

acting down when you are ill can also make your visitors depressed, which can lead to you even feeling worse

I have never heard an ill person praised for how well she expressed fear or grief or was openly sad. On the contrary, ill persons feel a need to apologize if they show any emotions other than laughter. Occasional tears may be passed off as the ill person's need to "let go"; the tears are categorized as temporary outbursts instead of understood as part of an ongoing emotion. Sustained "negative" emotions are out of place. If a patient shows too much sadness, he must be depressed, and "depression" is a treatable medical disease.

Too few people, whether medical staff, family, or friends, seem willing to accept the possibility that depression may be the ill person's most appropriate response to the situation. I am not recommending depression, but I do want to suggest that at some moments even fairly deep depression must be accepted as part of the experience of illness.

A couple of days before my mother-in-law died, she shared a room with a woman who was also being treated for cancer. My mother-in-law was this woman's second dying roommate, and the woman was seriously ill herself. I have no doubt that her diagnosis of clinical depression was accurate. The issue is how the medical staff responded to her depression. Instead of trying to understand it as a reasonable response to her situation, her doctors treated her with antidepressant drugs.

poor woman

When a hospital psychologist came to visit her, his questions were designed only to evaluate her "mental status." What day is it? Where are you and what floor are you on? Who is Prime Minister? and so forth. His sole interest was whether the dosage of antidepressant drug was too high, upsetting her "cognitive orientation." The hospital needed her to be mentally competent so she would remain a "good patient" requiring little extra care; it did not need her emotions. No one attempted to explore her fears with her. No one asked what it was like to have two roommates die within a couple of days of each other, and how this affected her own fear of death. No one was willing to witness her experience.

What makes me saddest is seeing the work ill persons do to sustain this "cheerful patient" image. A close friend of ours, dying of cancer, seriously wondered how her condition could be getting worse, since she had brought homemade cookies to the treatment center whenever she had chemotherapy. She believed there had to be a causal connection between attitude and physical improvement. From early childhood on we are taught that attitude and effort count. "Good citizenship" is supposed to bring us extra points. The nurses all said what a wonderful woman our friend was. She was the perfectly brave, positive, cheerful cancer patient. To me she was most wonderful at the end, when she grieved her illness openly, dropped her act, and clearly demonstrated her anger. She lived her illness as she chose, and by the time she was acting on her anger and sadness, she was too sick for me to ask her if she wished she had expressed more of those emotions earlier. I can only wonder what it had cost her to sustain her happy image for so long.

the whole fake-it-to-you-make-it scenario that we're all taught

When I tried to sustain a cheerful and tidy image, it cost me energy, which was scarce. It also cost me opportunities to express what *was* happening in my life with cancer and to understand that life. Finally, my attempts at a positive image diminished my relationships with others by preventing them from sharing my experience. But this image is all that many of those around an ill person are willing to see.

The other side of sustaining a "positive" image is denying that illness can end in death. Medical staff argue that patients who need to deny dying should be allowed to do so. The sad end of this process comes when the person is dying but has become too sick to express what he might now want to say to his loved ones, about his life and theirs. Then that person and his family are denied a final experience together; not all will choose this moment, but all have a right to it.

The medical staff do not have to be part of the tragedy of living with what was left unsaid. For them a patient who denies is one who is cheerful, makes few demands, and asks fewer questions. Some ill persons may need to deny, for reasons we cannot know. But it is too convenient for treatment providers to assume that the denial comes entirely from the patient, because this allows them not to recognize that they are cueing the patient. Labeling the ill person's behavior as denial describes it as a need of the patient, instead of understanding it as the patient's *response* to his situation. That situation, made up of the cues given by treatment providers and caregivers, is what shapes the ill person's behavior.

To be ill is to be dependent on medical staff, family, and friends. Since all these people value cheerfulness, the ill must summon up their energies to be cheerful. Denial may not be what they want or need, but it is what they perceive those around them wanting and needing. This is not the ill person's own denial, but rather his accommodation to the denial of others. When others around you are denying what is happening to you, denying it yourself can seem like your best deal.

To live among others is to make deals. We have to decide what support we need and what we must give others to get that support. Then we make our "best deal" of behavior to get what we need. This process is rarely a conscious one. It develops over a long time in so many experiences that it becomes the way we are, or what we call our personality. But behind much of what we call personality, deals are being made. In a crisis such as illness the terms of the deal rise to the surface and can be seen more clearly.

One incident can stand for all the deals I made during treatment. During my chemotherapy I had to spend three-day periods as an inpatient, receiving continuous drugs. In the three weeks or so between treatments I was examined weekly in the day-care part of the cancer center. Day care is a large room filled with easy chairs where patients sit while they are given briefer intravenous chemotherapy than mine. There are also beds, closely spaced with curtains between. Everyone can see everyone else and hear most of what is being said. Hospitals, however, depend on a myth of privacy. As soon as a curtain is pulled, that space is defined as private, and the patient is expected to answer all questions, no matter how intimate. The first time we went to day care, a young nurse interviewed Cathie and me to assess our "psychosocial" needs. In the middle of this medical bus station she began asking some reasonable questions. Were we experiencing dif-

[margin note, handwritten:] I wouldn't feel comfortable talking about intimate things in these conditions

ficulties at work because of my illness? Were we having any problems with our families? Were we getting support from them? These questions were precisely what a caregiver should ask. The problem was where they were being asked.

Our response to most of these questions was to lie. Without even looking at each other, we both understood that whatever problems we were having, we were not going to talk about them there. Why? To figure out our best deal, we had to assess the kind of support we thought we could get in that setting from that nurse. Nothing she did convinced us that what she could offer was equal to what we would risk by telling her the truth.

Admitting that you have problems makes you vulnerable, but it is also the only way to get help. Throughout my illness Cathie and I constantly weighed our need for help against the risk involved in making ourselves vulnerable. If we did not feel that support was forthcoming, we suppressed our need for expression. If we had expressed our problems and emotions in that very public setting, we would have been extremely vulnerable. If we had then received anything less than total support, it would have been devastating. The nurse showed no awareness or appreciation of how much her questions required us to risk, so we gave only a cheerful "no problems" response. That was all the setting seemed able to support.

Maybe we were wrong. Maybe the staff would have supported us if we had opened up our problems with others' responses to my illness, our stress trying to keep our jobs going, and our fears and doubts about treatment. We certainly were aware that our responses cut off that support. It was double or nothing; we chose safety. Ill persons face such choices constantly. We still believe we were right to keep quiet. If the staff had had real support to offer, they would have offered it in a setting that encouraged our response. When we were alone with nurses in an inpatient room, the questions they asked were those on medical history forms. In the privacy of that room the nurses were vulnerable to the emotions we might have expressed, so they asked no "psychosocial" questions.

no escape or distractions from troubling responses from patients in hospital

It was a lot of work for us to answer the day-care nurse's questions with a smile. Giving her the impression that we felt all right was draining, and illness and its care had drained us both already. But expending our energies this way seemed our best deal.

Anybody who wants to be a caregiver, particularly a professional, must not only have real support to offer but must also learn to convince the ill person that this support is there. My defenses have never been stronger than they were when I was ill. I have never watched others more closely or been more guarded around them. I needed others more than I ever have, and I was also most vulnerable to them. The behavior I worked to let others see was my most conservative estimate of what I thought they would support.

Again I can give no formula, only questions. To the ill person: How much is this best deal costing you in terms of emotional work? What are you compromising of your own expression of illness in order to present those around you with the cheerful appearance they want? What do you fear will happen if you act otherwise? And to those around the ill person: What cues are you giving the ill person that tell her how you want her to act? In what way is her behavior a response to your own? Whose denial, whose needs?

Fear and depression are a part of life. In illness there are no "negative emotions," only experiences that have to be lived through. What is needed in these moments is not denial but recognition. The ill person's suffering should be affirmed, whether or not it can be treated. What I wanted when I was most ill was the response, "Yes, we see your pain; we accept your fear." I needed others to recognize not only that I was suffering, but also that we had this suffering in common. I can accept that doctors and nurses sometimes fail to provide the correct treatment. But I cannot accept it when medical staff, family, and friends fail to recognize that they are equal participants in the process of illness. Their actions shape the behavior of the ill person, and their bodies share the potential of illness.

Those who make cheerfulness and bravery the price they require for support deny their own humanity. They deny that to be human is to be mortal, to become ill and die. Ill persons need others to share in recognizing with them the frailty of the human body. When others join the ill person in this recognition, courage and cheer may be the result, not as an appearance to be worked at, but as a spontaneous expression of a common emotion.

Chemotherapy and Adventure

GOING INTO chemotherapy, I had every hope and just as many fears. Chemotherapy is effective for testicular cancer patients about 80 percent of the time, depending on how far the cancer has progressed. Given the delays in my diagnosis, my odds were probably not that good. But no matter how good or bad the odds were, they were only odds. Getting testicular cancer in the first place did not make me feel lucky. Thus medicine's attitude of "You've got it made" became irritating. I restrained myself from asking physicians or nurses how they would feel if told they had a 20 percent chance of not making it home safe that night. The good odds supported my hopes, but the way I was told these odds carried the message that my fears were not legitimate.

The idea of good odds is one of the ways medicine defines chemotherapy as simply an "incident." The medical staff's descriptions of chemotherapy always minimized the suffering. One day when my side effects were particularly bad I was lying in a bed in day care, doing what patients do best, which is wait. On the other side of the curtain a physician was giving another patient the same introduction to chemotherapy speech I remembered from a couple of months earlier. Chemotherapy was presented as merely a transitory inconvenience: no need to take much time off from work, there will be hair loss but nothing else serious, just a couple of months, and so on. I had a wicked desire to pull back the curtain and say, "Yes, and you'll look like this." That patient did not need to know everything in advance; still, he had a right to be told enough to allow him to do some realistic planning. More important, he had a right to have affirmed that what he was going through was no small thing. Instead he was being cued not to take his experience seriously, and that is what I wish I could have changed.

Many people have far longer chemotherapies than I had, with far worse chances of recovery. It may become easy for those who work in cancer centers to think of chemotherapy for testicular cancer as merely a transitory inconvenience. Unfortunately, this attitude denies ill persons the validity and importance of what we experience. The three months of chemotherapy seemed like a lifetime to me, in part because of my fear that it might be the end of my life, but also because of the suffering I acknowledged and the adventure I found.

The chemotherapy used for testicular cancer was first described to me as one of the "most aggressive" treatments given. I had this image of five brawny guys throwing me on a bed and starting an IV. The aggressiveness, of course, refers to the toxicity of the drugs and the severity of their side effects. Although hair loss is the side effect most often associated with chemotherapy, far more discomforting were the nausea, gum soreness, constipation, and, perhaps most intense although brief, the burning pain while urinating. A more important side effect is the destruction of the white cells that are the basis of the immune system. Although this causes no discomfort, it increases the person's vulnerability to sickness; I lived in fear that sickness would disrupt the schedule of chemotherapy.

Beyond these specific side effects, chemotherapy leaves the body feeling wrecked. This is not surprising, since it is nothing more than toxic drugs killing the body's cells. How it made me feel can be compared with the effect my two operations had on me. Even though I had no conscious memory of pain while under anesthetic, my body retained a sense of what had been done to it. Something had happened to me, and even if I couldn't quite remember it, I knew it had been awful. Chemotherapy involved no real pain, but my body again knew something awful was being done to it.

If anyone reading this book is about to have chemotherapy, she should realize that these side effects vary depending on the individual and the treatment. Improvements are being made in the drugs to counter the side effects, and the treatments themselves change. The details of my treatment are part of my own story, *not* a guide to what others can expect.

Each chemotherapy treatment was administered over three days, during which I was an inpatient in the cancer center. I was given different drugs intravenously according to a specific time schedule. The sequencing had to be exact, because each drug kills cancer cells at different stages of their development. The number of treatments varies. Not long before my illness patients were usually given six treatments, but I had three. Some recent research suggests that one treatment may be fully effective. The drugs seem to do as much the first time as they are ever going to. As attractive as the idea of having only one treatment is, I was not sure, even during chemotherapy, that I wanted to be the first to get less than the usual course. I had lived with the fear of cancer for so long that finally being treated gave me a sense of security.

Between treatments I went home, returning to the cancer center each week for blood tests and medication to relieve side effects. I felt the worst physical effects from the second day after I got home until about a week later. Within a week I could read without nausea, though still without much concentration. My appetite returned with a vengeance, and my mouth soreness lessened enough to allow me to eat. In the remaining ten days or so before my next treatment I lived as normal a life as I could with constant medical appointments and no immune system. About the time I began to feel fairly good, my white blood cell count was high enough for another round of chemotherapy. We began again.

Two weeks after each treatment I also had a CAT (computerized axial tomography) scan to determine if the tumors along my back had decreased in size. The progress of this decrease determined when chemotherapy would stop, so I did not know if my third treatment was my last until the scan two weeks afterward. After a certain point the tumors did not shrink any further, and my cancer center assumed that what was left was scar tissue. I was scanned for a year after treatment to confirm that no tumors were growing.

The CAT scans were not pleasant. In movies the patient is wafted through a high-tech donut with lights flashing all round. In reality it is less entertaining. The night before a scan I had to take massive laxatives to empty my intestines. At most I got two hours of sleep. During the scan I had a barium enema, and sometimes an intravenous needle in my arm put another contrast fluid into the circulatory system. The scans are obviously less "invasive" than surgery, but during the procedure I felt invaded enough. With the enema and the IV going, you lie absolutely still for about thirty minutes, holding your arms above your head while passing through an X-ray that takes a sequence of cross-sectional pictures. These provide an exact image of the internal organs and, in my case, tumors.

Chemotherapy has a terrible reputation, but my own aggressive treatment had no special horrors. It was a series of mundane discomforts, one after another, with no rest. The drugs and the hospital rooms induced a sense of claustrophobia, heightened by the two IV lines that ran into me, one for the chemotherapy drugs themselves and the other for anti-nausea drugs. The latter were effective, but they left me too disoriented for real conversation. I slept irregularly. When I was awake, time passed in minutes. The drugs dissociated me from my body's usual feedback; drugged, I lived in an "it." Mostly it felt restless but also as though moving would make me seriously nauseated.

These IVs did not involve needles because I had undergone a second operation to install a "central line" or permanent catheter. One end of a tube was placed directly in my heart, and the other end passed under the skin up by the collarbone and down across the chest, exiting just below the ribs, with about a foot of tubing coming out. When I was not having an IV, the tubing was taped to my chest. Catheters for single IVs sit just below the skin, but I was going to be given such large doses of drugs that a two-IV model was necessary. The purpose of the central line was to prevent veins from collapsing because of the toxicity of the chemotherapy drugs, and also to provide for better dispersion of the drugs through the body.

Thus my three months of chemotherapy were spent with a foot of tubing hanging out of my chest. The line became part of my body, but the body was no longer entirely mine. The line was a symbol of cancer that I wore on my body; even when I felt pretty good, there it was, reminding me of all the aspects of cancer. I was vulnerable because it carried the risk of infection, and I was dependent on it during treatment. Through it chemotherapy drugs went in and blood samples came out.

The line was another flag planted by the medical system on my body. I resented it as much as I needed it. My tolerance for pain had been chipped away, first by the tumors that woke me at night and later by such mundane hospital annoyances as being wakened each morning for blood tests. Blood tests are no big thing, but when you are woken every day by someone sticking a needle into your arm several times, this too drains your resistance to discomfort.

I needed the line not only for relief from pain, but also as a way of displacing my larger fears about cancer. I was able to refocus these fears — whether chemotherapy was working, how long it would go on — onto the daily problems of managing the line. If cancer itself was too much to worry about, I could worry instead about the line. Because the exit site is an open wound, it could become infected. The line might malfunction and fail to draw blood properly, although I had no such problems with it. But I never had full use of my right arm; too much movement would cause the line to pull.

The line also refocused the relationship Cathie and I had fallen into. By the time it was installed, the hospital had pretty well taken me over. Although Cathie was usually with me during physician's visits, the doctors and nurses never acknowledged her presence. Medical staff talked to me even if they found it difficult to make eye contact with me; they treated Cathie like a nonperson. She and I observed this and even joked about it, but it wore on us. Hospitals separate physical treatment from emotional care; caregivers are treated like an optional luxury, pleasant for the patient to have around but not necessary to treatment. Cathie and I were having a hard time resisting being split into patient and visitor.

Physical care requires emotional support, and emotional support needs physical involvement, which the line provided. The exit site had to be disinfected and bandaged daily, and during the intervals between chemotherapy treatments, the line had to be flushed with saline solution. Cathie took over the disinfecting, flushing, and bandaging, and these tasks became a daily ritual between us. We laughed that it was "our special time" together, but those moments of quiet in a hectic life were a gift. My illness had not decreased the normal demands of our lives, particularly of her life, and had added many demands of its own. Soon the procedure with the line became routine, and we were able to talk while Cathie went through the motions. Illness can crowd out talk. The time spent maintaining the line each day, even if it was yet another of cancer's demands, was one way of finding new terms for our relationship. When I went back to being an inpatient, Cathie and I joked about how much better her antiseptic procedures were than those of the nurses who dressed the line. At least between ourselves, she was no longer a visitor.

*

Chemotherapy accentuates the basic challenge presented by illness: how to continue to live when your life has been altered so radically. It turned life into a bizarre roller coaster of destruction and recovery, repeated three times. A new side effect would require a different medication, or some other worry would need attention. But behind these mundane problems lurked the only real issue: would it be effective? Would I be one of the lucky 80 percent who come out alive? And behind the danger that I might die was the danger that even while I was alive I might be worn away by what was happening.

The danger of chemotherapy is that you may lose the sense of value in your life; you may fade into the claustrophobia and passivity of treatment and become so obsessed with details of bodily care that your mind shares the numbness of your body. The opportunity is to discover new sources of value in familiar things too often ignored. Although my side effects were worse when I was at home, I could live with them because of what it meant to be at home. Getting out of the hospital always seemed like a rebirth. Hospitals deprive the senses; outside I was aware of real air and colors and textures, variations of light and the noise of a normal world going about its business. At home there were cards and calls from friends and family. I heard from people I had not seen in years and was surprised they even knew I had cancer. These messages in particular gave me what I think ill persons need most, a sense that many others, more than you can think of, care deeply that you live. Most of all, home was where Cathie and I could be together in a place that was ours.

But at home as in the hospital, the ill person is eventually alone with illness. Then what was I to think about all that was happening to me? What was I to make of myself, vulnerable, dependent, my body often unable to eat or excrete? I never thought up any answers to these questions, but some answers found me. Unsought and unexpected, a sense of adventure came to me from two very different places.

In our living room we have a lithograph that was given to me years ago, a poster by Marc Chagall for a show in Paris in the 1960s. The theme of the show was Chagall's biblical art, and in the lithograph Jacob is being blessed by the angel. On days when I was able to do little more than sit, I watched the afternoon light pass through the room and gazed at the Chagall. Here is the biblical text:

> And Jacob was left alone; and there wrestled a man with him until the breaking of the day.
>
> And when he saw that he prevailed not against him, he touched the hollow of his thigh; and the hollow of Jacob's thigh was out of joint, as he wrestled with him.
>
> And he said, Let me go, for the day breaketh. And he said, I will not let thee go, except thou bless me.
>
> And he said unto him, What is thy name? And he said, Jacob.
>
> And he said, thy name shall be called no more Jacob, but Israel: for as a prince hast thou power with God and with men, and hast prevailed.
>
> And Jacob asked him, and said, Tell me, I pray thee, thy name. And he said, Wherefore is it that thou dost ask after my name? And he blessed him there.
>
> And Jacob called the name of the place Peniel: for I have seen God face to face, and my life is preserved.

And as he passed over Peniel the sun rose upon him, and he
halted upon his thigh. (Genesis 32:24–30)

Stories we tell ourselves about what is happening to us are
dangerous because they are powerful. Stories come to us from
many sources; some we seek, many happen without our notice, others impose themselves on our lives. We have to choose
carefully which stories to live with, which to use to answer the
question of what is happening to us. Jacob's wrestling became
a story I lived with as part of my personal mythology of illness.
This is what it is to be ill: to wrestle through the long night,
injured, and if you prevail until the sun rises, to receive a
blessing. Through Jacob's story, illness became an adventure.

Other stories found their way into this personal mythology
of illness as adventure. It was the autumn when Paul Simon's
album "Graceland" was popular. Pop music at its best has an
openness that allows the listener to believe it was written just
for him. A story that is anyone's can become yours. As I sat
pumped full of chemicals, my immune system as close to gone
as the doctors dared drive it, Simon's "The Boy in the Bubble"
became mine.

> These are the days of miracles and wonder
> This is the long distance call
> The way the camera follows us in slo-mo
> The way we look to us all
> The way we look to a distant constellation
> That's dying in a corner of the sky
> These are the days of miracles and wonder
> And don't cry baby don't cry
> Don't cry

It seemed easy to cry during those days. But between Jacob's angel and Simon's miracles and wonder, I found a sense of adventure in illness. My body was a toxic waste dump, but it was also living a miracle. Twenty years before, maybe even ten, I would have been dying instead of getting chemotherapy. Now the ultimate slo-mo of the CAT scan cameras showed the tumors shrinking. My existence was a wonder, living it an adventure. I could believe in prevailing until the sun rose. The blessing was that I was seeing life, face to face.

The Struggle Is Not a Fight

PEOPLE with other diseases are just plain sick; those with cancer "fight" it. During my heart trouble no one suggested I fight my heart, but one of the first things I was told about cancer was, "You have to fight." Read any set of obituaries. People die of cancer after a "valiant battle" or a "long bout." Government research programs are "wars" on cancer. Newspaper stories that refer to poverty, crime, and drug abuse as "cancers" reflect society's attitude toward cancer as the dreaded other. Against this other, combat is the only appropriate response. But I do not believe illness should be lived as a fight.

The fight metaphor does capture something of what living with illness is like. Cathie and I talked about cancer as a life during wartime. We did not mean we were waging a war against the enemy, cancer. Rather we were searching for words to describe lives that had been overrun. We thought of ourselves as civilians whose home had become a battlefield. Demands and crises followed one after the other so fast that we felt buffeted. As soon as we worked through the emotions of one crisis we were "hit" by another, ranging from a new side effect of chemotherapy to a feared infection of my line. Medical appointments conflicted with the demands of our jobs. As someone put it, illness is one damn thing after another. Pervading all of it, always, is the fear of dying. So life during wartime seemed an appropriate description.

But our talk never suggested that we were fighting cancer. We never thought of "the cancer" as a thing to be fought. That would have personified it, and it is this personification I object to. Cancer is not some entity separate from yourself. As I lay in my hospital room awaiting surgery, I had to find some way to understand these tumors inside me. Were they something alien, smuggled in from outside and not really part of me? Or were they as much a part of me as my brain and muscles?

Most people opt for the tumor-as-alien. At the extreme, Ronald Reagan's well-known statement about his cancer, "I don't have cancer. I had something inside of me that had cancer in it, and it was removed," sums up this unwillingness to understand cancer as part of oneself. I only hope this served Reagan well. For myself, I had cancer.

The tumors may have been a painful part of me, they may have threatened my life, but they were still me. They were part of a body that would not function much longer unless it changed, but that body was still who I was. I could never split my body into two warring camps: the bad guy tumors opposed to the naturally healthy me. There was only one me, one body, tumors and all. Accepting that I was still one body brought me a great sense of relief.

The tumors had to go if the body was to survive, but this was the body's problem. My consciousness could not make

experiential duality of pain

the tumors go away any more than it had brought them. Consciously I could only wonder at the body and accept its wisdom. I could desire to live, but life itself was more than I could take responsibility for. As soon as I gave up fighting myself and let my body change according to its wisdom — with some additional direction from surgery and chemotherapy — I felt far more peaceful. There was no fight, only the possibility of change. Making this possibility real involved suffering and struggle, but not fighting. Thinking of tumors as enemies and the body as a battlefield is not a gentle attitude toward oneself, and ill persons have only enough energy for gentleness. Aggression is misplaced energy. You may feel anger because of the way you are treated, but that is different from fighting yourself.

Though I did not personify my tumors, it seemed useful to visualize them. This process had nothing to do with fighting cancer. I simply allowed images of the tumors to appear, with as little conscious direction as possible, and visualized them disappearing. Actually I visualized my white blood cells more often than my tumors. In normal times white cells "kill" the cancer cells the body constantly produces. I imagined the white cells, but an image of them attacking the tumors never came to me. They were simply there, on guard, standing silhouetted on mountain cliffs. My imagination gave the white cells the form of ancient Greek soldiers, perhaps because my white cell count reminded me of the number of Greeks at the battle of Marathon, a word that has particular connotations for me as a runner.

I had learned many times that running a marathon is a struggle but it cannot be a fight. You cannot fight for twenty-six miles; it's too far. At least for a middle-aged recreational runner the trick in marathon running is to coddle the body. If you treat yourself as gently as possible, your body's energy will unfold over the distance. In the far reaches you may realize sources of energy you never knew the body had. The body knows how to run; you have to learn to let it.

During cancer I tried to let my body do what it wanted with the tumors. The white cells, my Greek guards, were there, watching. The tumors had no identity, no faces, hardly even shapes. Flaccid and without purpose, they were vulnerable. They had no basis for survival. It wasn't necessary to "attack" them; they simply disappeared. The tumors were super-fluous. My life was ready to move on and had no time for them.

I confess that I did ask myself how the tumors had gotten there to begin with. I do not recommend such thinking. It seems better to believe that cancer just happens. But at the time I could not resist asking "why me?" And this question led me to a sense of past inadequacy. A woman I know who has ovarian cancer believes that it was caused by an antinausea drug she took when she was pregnant. Unlike most of us, she can ask herself "why me?" and find answers that are not fantasies of self-blame. But for those who do not have such a direct physiological cause, the answer to "why me?" is bound to involve guilt. As the prayer I learned as a child in church said, "We have left undone those things which we ought to have done, And we have done those things which we ought not to have done, And" — here's the punchline — "there is no health in us." What terrible words to put in the mind of a child! It becomes all too easy for an ill person to work backward: If there is no health in me, then I must have done something wrong or at least left something undone.

This kind of confessional thinking led me to all sorts of regrets. It is proper to meditate on how you have lived so that you can become the person you want to be. But it is a sad mistake to believe that cancer is caused by something you have or have not done. To believe my own inadequacies were so spectacular that they gave me cancer is just vanity.

As a bodily process, cancer "just happened" to me. The explanations I like best are fairly medical. During my embryonic development, some of the cellular processes went wrong. Perhaps they went wrong in a way that would produce testicular cancer no matter what else happened to me. Perhaps this cellular time bomb was waiting for some stress or some virus or some combination of toxins we don't understand yet. Maybe someday the process will be controlled, just as someday we may understand the subtle and indirect ways that the mind can influence both the disease and the cure of the body. But at our present level of knowledge, cancer of the type I had just happens.

But if I did not do anything that caused cancer, neither am I just a pawn in some random draw of bodies destined to become diseased. As soon as cancer happened to me, not just to anyone, it ceased to be random. I am a bodily process, but I am also a consciousness, with a will and a history and a capacity to focus my thoughts and energies. The bodily process and the consciousness do not oppose each other; what illness teaches is their unity. The mind gives meaning to what happens in the body, but the mind also thinks through the body it is a part of. The mind does not simply contemplate itself in a body with cancer. As cancer reshapes that body, the mind changes in response to the disease's effects. Pain taught me the body's power to shape thinking. But my thinking was shaping the pain even as it was being shaped by that pain — the circle is unbroken.

Illness is a physical process and an experience, each shaping the other. The physical process just happens to me; the experience is my responsibility. What my body does in the last five miles of a marathon just happens, but what just happens has been shaped by a lifetime of choosing to use that body in particular ways. In my body's will I recognize my will, and it goes beyond consciousness, while still including that consciousness.

We cannot fight cancer or tumors. We can only trust the body's will and get as much medical help as we can. We form the body's will through years of conscious acts, but in the end what finally happens just happens. I still believe there is great health in us, but we also die some day. I am not powerful enough to feel either guilty for getting sick or proud of getting well. I can only take what happens to me and continue to look for possibilities of how to live.

Writing about the value of not fighting takes me back to Jacob wrestling with the angel. The story is about a man fighting for his soul, but we have to look carefully at how this fight proceeds. For me, the other whom Jacob wrestles is himself. Jacob's personal history is checkered, to say the least. He begins by stealing his father's blessing from his older brother, Esau, who rightly should have had it. Jacob is then tricked by his father-in-law into marrying the wrong sister. After various deceptions and escapes, Jacob is finally alone. At that moment in his life, he could easily believe there were two of him: his good self and his "dark twin," who stole Esau's blessing and generated the other troubles that followed. This dark twin is the character whom various mythologies call the trickster. Jacob has to decide which side of him will prevail, the servant of God or his dark twin, the trickster.

The wrestling is a struggle but not a fight. Jacob wins not by defeating his darker side, but by realizing that the other he is contesting shares the face of God. Jacob does not overcome his opponent; instead he finds divinity in him. The outcome of the wrestling match is twofold. Jacob leaves with a wound: "The sun rose upon him, and he halted upon his thigh." He also gains a blessing: The servant of God wins for himself the prize the trickster first stole, but perhaps the blessing is that now the two have become one. Wounded, Jacob becomes whole. Whole, he is renamed.

Illness is not a fight against an other, but it is a long struggle. Some prevail by continuing to live; some prevail in dying. Those who are ill and those who witness illness can only have faith in the wholeness of either outcome. Faith must displace will, just as struggling with cancer must displace fighting against it.

Being ill is a perpetual balancing of faith and will. I find this quality of faith in the stories of Jacob and other Old Testament characters attempting to serve what they call God's will. It is a will outside of themselves that, in my language, just happens to them. When Moses is asked to lead the Hebrews from Egypt, or when Abraham is told to sacrifice Isaac, or when Noah builds an ark, they must accept what just seems to happen. This quality of acceptance is what I call faith.

But faith is hardly resignation. Acceptance requires each to achieve something. Jacob most actively wrestles with a paradox: a will that is his but is other than his own. He discovers that even his trickster self has the face of God, and in this paradoxical discovery he becomes whole.

Diseases are not messages from some god, nor is illness a test of faith. These ideas are among the dangers of a mythology that also has opportunities. The opportunity is to recognize that although illness just happens, we can organize its experience to make our lives meaningful. We can have both a faith that allows us to accept whatever just happens and at the same time a will to bring about the change we desire. Thus I find no contradiction between leaving illness to the body's will and seeking medical help. We are most faithful when active, just as we struggle best when we do not fight.

Stigma

WHENEVER I told someone I had cancer I felt myself tighten as I said it. Saying the word "cancer," my body began to defend itself. This did not happen when I told people I was having heart problems. A heart attack was simply bad news. But I never stopped thinking that cancer said something about my worth as a person. This difference between heart attack and cancer is stigma. A stigma is, literally, a sign on the surface of the body marking it as dangerous, guilty, and unclean. Stigmas began as judicial punishments in the form of notched ears, brandings, and other visible mutilations of the body. These marks allowed those who came into contact with the stigmatized person to see whom they were dealing with. The stigmatized were expected to go to the margins of society and hide their spoiled bodies. The causes of stigmatization have changed, but the hiding has not.

My heart attack damaged my body but did not stigmatize it. I became short of breath while doing tasks that were normal for a man my age. This was inconvenient and embarrassing but not stigmatizing. The damaged body only fails to perform properly; the stigmatized body contaminates its surroundings. During my heart problems I could no longer participate in certain activities; during cancer I felt I had no right to be among others. As much as I disliked being in the hospital, at least there I felt I belonged. I knew this was foolish. I didn't belong in the hospital; I was hiding there. Ill persons hide in many ways. Some begin to call cancer "c.a.," "the big C," or other euphemisms. I called it cancer, but as I said it I felt that tightness.

Heart attacks are invisible on the body's surface. To myself and to others, I looked no different. One wears cancer. My own visible stigmas were hair loss and my intravenous line. The line created a bulge over my chest, but I could conceal it. Getting dressed each day became an exercise in concealment. I wore shirts that were heavy and loose fitting and equally loose sweaters. A tie under the sweater added some bulk, and a sport coat further obscured the contours of my body. The question, of course, is why I wanted to hide the line from others. The sad answer is that I experienced the visible signs of cancer as defects not just in my appearance, but in myself.

The visible sign most closely associated with cancer is hair loss. Alopecia, or baldness, is caused not by cancer itself but by its treatment. Chemotherapy is not very discriminating. Cancer cells divide rapidly, but so do the cells of hair follicles, the intestinal lining, and gums. The drugs destroy cells in all these areas, creating their particular side effects. Thus there is truth to the folk wisdom that baldness indicates chemotherapy is working. Even knowing this, my enthusiasm for losing my hair was qualified.

My hair fell out several days after my first chemotherapy

treatment. First it lost its texture and became thin, then the hair on the sides of my head rubbed off while I was washing it. I was left with a patchy-looking mohawk. It was almost Halloween, but I resisted the temptation to turn my appearance into a punk costume.

Some people try to preserve what hair they have for as long as they can. I thought I looked stranger with some hair than I would with none. Also we got tired of cleaning out the tub and drain every time I took a shower; hot water speeds up the hair loss. So Cathie helped me shave off the rest of my hair, which was truly a labor of love. That shaving marked my full passage into another stage of illness, and it was a sad thing. The loss of hair has to be mourned; it is another break with the younger self you no longer are.

To be completely bald at my age was a bit unusual, but it was not in itself stigmatizing. I had never thought of hair loss as one of life's great problems. But losing my hair all at once was traumatic, even if my age and gender reduced the trauma. For women and some younger males the loss would be different, but not entirely different. The actual hair loss bothered me less than what this loss meant. Cancer made baldness into a stigma; I imagined others seeing me as a cancer "victim." Baldness was a reduction to the passivity of a victim, a patient, or a sufferer. Even a woman who normally wore a wig would feel this stigma, given her present reason for that wig.

The first week without hair was physically unpleasant and emotionally difficult. My newly bald head was extremely sensitive to touch and cold. Even a pillowcase felt rough to skin that had never been exposed to direct touch. I had to sleep on a soft towel. The normal drafts in our house felt like a wind tunnel on my head. This physical unpleasantness lasted only a few days, but the stigma remained.

I took to wearing a hat. In part this was for warmth; November turned cold that year, and I quickly realized how much insulation even short hair provides. But I also used the hat to give others a chance to adjust their reactions as they saw that I had no hair around the sides and then realized I had none at all. I grew fond of my hat, but I also needed its protection. I had a dark fantasy, which many stigmatized persons have in one form or another. My fear was that someday, somewhere, someone would see my bald head and scream, "Oh my god, he has cancer!" Looking back on that time, I was the one who was screaming.

Gradually I began leaving the hat off, at first around the office and then at concerts and such. But I did not lose my sense of stigma until after chemotherapy ended. As I became confident that I was in remission, my self-consciousness disappeared. The only time I actually heard anyone talking about my baldness was about six weeks after the end of chemotherapy, when my head was developing a five o'clock shadow. I was standing in a line and heard a woman telling a child that maybe I was in the army, where they cut their hair very short. I smiled to myself. By then baldness was nothing more than the absence of hair. The cause of the stigma had disappeared when I went into remission and was no longer a cancer patient; the visible sign had lost its meaning. I was just a bald, middle-aged college professor who could still pass as an army recruit.

During active treatment I never found a way of dealing with my sense of stigma. Like the experience of pain, stigma ended before I resolved it. I do not think I could ever have resolved it alone. If the person with cancer can believe that other people's phobias about cancer are their problem, fine, but this thought brings little comfort to those who feel stigmatized. Telling people to hang tough only works for those who already are.

The idea that cancer represents a defect in the ill person's identity does not go away easily. Society imposes this idea on us every day in subtle ways. The newspapers recently carried a story about an advertising model who once portrayed the macho image of the Winston man in that tobacco company's advertisements. He quit smoking and now works for health promotion groups that are trying to eliminate cigarettes. One reason for the change was that his brother got lung cancer. In the article the man's visit to his brother in the hospital was reduced to a description of seeing all these "guys without hair." The loss, suffering, and fear that go with cancer were reduced to the most visible symbol, the bald head. Of course, pain and death are too much for our imaginations; hair loss is immediately understood. It becomes the part of cancer we can grasp when the whole overwhelms us.

The newspaper story subtly reconfirms the stigma of baldness. It links a voluntary behavior, smoking, to cancer, whose dominant sign is baldness. Wrong action produces the disease, and the disease is reduced to its visual sign. I admire what the former model is doing, and I support the antismoking message of the story. But we are left with an unfortunate moral allegory: the man saved from the damnation of smoking by seeing his brother's fall into cancer. It's a health promotion version of Dickens's "A Christmas Carol," with the brother as Marley's ghost, telling the Winston man to reform or end up like him. Since the days of notched ears, the power of stigma has fed on seeing the body's condition as an expression of morality, and this linkage is virtually irresistible to our thinking.

The story is one example of how society defines stigmas. Because AIDS is now the most stigmatized disease, persons with AIDS understand how society imposes stigmas on individuals. I believe all ill persons, particularly those with cancer, have much to learn from persons with AIDS. Because many of them had been politically active in the gay rights movement, they knew that society's response to disease is a political issue. They first insisted on being called "persons with AIDS" instead of patients, victims, or sufferers. The shift in language marks a change to thinking of oneself as active, not passive; thus I write about persons with cancer, except when they are specifically patients. At times a person with cancer may be a patient or a victim (of a carcinogenic drug, for example), or a sufferer. But what matters most, no matter what you call yourself or are called, is that you remain foremost a person, actively living your life.

Resisting stigmatization requires more than individual will. Ill persons who cannot brush off stigmatization as someone else's problem need to organize themselves. The prospect of hanging tough against stigma may not be comforting to one who must do it alone, but as a group people can hang tough. The problem is that organizations of ill persons are often not supported by institutional medicine. In some cancer centers self-help organizations are restricted or prohibited from visiting patients to make them aware of what support is available. Because organizations of ill persons often define treatment issues as political, they make demands that hospitals do not want to hear. Institutions find it easier to manage patients who think of themselves as isolated and are thus passive. Society is obsessed with "health," but it prefers to keep ill persons on its margins, making them as invisible as possible. When people are stigmatized, they hide themselves.

Cancer can do terrible things to the body, but so can other diseases. Cultural historians tell us that for at least a century cancer has been North Americans' most feared disease. This fear is explained only partially by either actual rates of cancer incidence and mortality or by the physical suffering it causes. Society, not the disease itself, makes cancer as dreaded as it is. A culture in which people are unwilling to speak the name of the disease obviously has a special fear. We do not call heart attack "h.a." Cancer alone is mythologized as some savage god, whose very name will invoke its presence. If the name of cancer is unspeakable, what evil does the person with cancer believe can be brought by his presence? Newspaper stories and political speeches use cancer as the metaphor for all the worst that can happen. The ill person then becomes the bearer of these horrors. Just as I tried to hide my intravenous line under my coat, persons with cancer want to hide their disease. Never have I tried so hard to be invisible.

To lose the sense of stigma, persons with cancer must come in from the margins and be visible. Organizations of ill persons are one form of visibility; I hope this book will be another. Stigmatization will be overcome only when we learn to witness the experience of cancer, not hide it. Every attempt to hide cancer, every euphemism, every concealment, reconfirms that the stigma is real and deserved. When I heard that woman explaining my shaved hair to a child, it was a personal victory for me to be able to smile. It would have been a social victory if I had walked over and said, "No, actually I'm recovering from cancer, but it's all right; cancer's only another disease, and diseases are only human." That would have broken the cycle of stigma.

Denial and Affirmation

Pᴇᴏᴘʟᴇ ᴅɪᴅ ɴᴏᴛ ᴀᴄᴛ that differently toward me while I had cancer, they only exaggerated how they had always acted. The compassionate ones became more loving, the generous more giving, the ill at ease more defensive. The bullies were peskier than usual, and the ones who were always too busy remained busy. Some people whom I expected to be supportive denied that I was ill at all; medical staff denied that I was anything but the disease. Others affirmed that although I was ill and illness counted, we still had a relationship. These denials and affirmations were not always easy to recognize as they happened. Denials can be subtle; after being with someone I would feel bad and not be sure why.

But illness also exaggerated the ways I acted toward others. I needed other people desperately but, feeling stigmatized, I was cautious of them. One day I would express closeness, the next day distance. My behavior caused others to exaggerate their responses to me, and in my perception of them I exaggerated their actions still further. Even the strongest relationships came under stress. This is how the ill person experiences others during illness: subtle denials, strained affirmations.

The most subtle denials may be those of cancer itself. One day Cathie and I were appreciating a nurse's interest in us until she said to Cathie, "Oh, your mother died of c.a. too." And there it was again: another refusal to say the dreaded c-word. She undoubtedly thought she was protecting us; nurses are very keen on "not upsetting the patient." But if that is the explanation, why do nurses use these euphemisms among themselves when no patients are around to become upset? Cathie and I have both worked on the "professional" side of hospitals enough to know that the patient's presence does not determine how nurses speak, or don't speak, of cancer.

More important than the nurse's motive was that I experienced her "c.a." as a denial. I was waiting to be examined because I feared I was having a recurrence of cancer. Although I did not welcome it, I was working hard to think that if cancer was happening again, I would live with it. Then the nurse's refusal to say the word "cancer" told me that what might be happening to my body was too awful to be called by its proper name. I was suddenly ashamed of what might be wrong with me. In the silencing of the word "cancer," I as a person with cancer was also silenced. It was the same silencing I had experienced when Cathie told me about the nurse who referred to me as the "seminoma in 53." She denied that I existed as anything more than the disease. Now even the disease was unspeakable. In that nurse's "c.a." I disappeared.

Suffering also is denied. Those who provide treatment give patients cues as to the emotions that are appropriate to express. Because patients are dependent on medical staff, they tend to accept these cues. Nurses and physicians cue patients to deny their own experience when they compare one patient's suffering to that of someone who is "much worse off." Comparisons deny the uniqueness of each individual's experience. As losses, disfigurements, pains are compared, a standard emerges against which the suffering of each individual is measured. Compared to the suffering of the "worst case," my experiences are devalued. This logic makes it possible to find the one person, first in the hospital, eventually in the world, who is *the* worst off. Only that "designated complainer" would have any right to express discomfort, unhappiness, fear, or any other "negative" emotion.

Ill persons deserve better. My suffering cannot be compared to yours or to anyone else's; it can only be witnessed for what it is. When I talk to other persons with cancer, we do not compare frequency of nausea, duration of hair loss, or length of scars. Persons with cancer respect each other's experiences. They recognize that having cancer is no small thing.

Medical staff who make comparisons are trapped by a belief that unless they can do something to reduce the bodily suffering, they have failed as professionals. Continuing suffering threatens them, so they deny it exists. What they cannot treat, the patient is not allowed to experience. Physicians and nurses often forget that when treatment runs out, there can still be care. Simply recognizing suffering for what it is, regardless of whether it can be treated, is care.

Professionals can and do care, but when they do they are acting a bit unprofessional. When my diagnosis was uncertain, one medical resident spent some time just letting me talk. Our talk wasn't related to treatment; he listened to my fears and shared his own. Later his supervisor advised him that once symptoms and history have been elicited, further talk with patients is considered unproductive. Sadly, the standard of what is "professional" often denies the opportunity for care.

The only way I could get my surgeon, a seasoned professional, to talk to me about the details of and alternatives to the operation he was planning (which was never carried out and would have been unnecessary) was to refuse to sign the consent form. In effect I denied his denial. We then had a long conversation. His knowledge and experience helped me, but this help came only after I had hit him with the only two-by-four a patient has. Or perhaps, in the inverted world of hospitals, my not signing permitted him to have the kind of contact he would like to have with patients but cannot justify.

The denials an ill person faces do not stop with treatment. The institutions for which most of us work deny that people have bodies and that life requires attention to these bodies. Institutions consider bodies only as resources for production, not as lives being lived. Thus the sympathy an ill person receives has institutional limits. While I was in active treatment, the university where I work was most solicitous. Arrangements were made for others to teach my classes when I was too ill, and my department sent flowers to the hospital. People I worked with expressed concern for me.

But as soon as treatment ended, the other institutional face appeared. Some of the same people now asked for the work I was supposed to have been doing. It didn't count that I had been ill; in the annual assessment written about each faculty member, the time of my illness was described as showing a "lack of scholarly productivity." I had to remind the administrator who wrote the report to specify that this lack was due to illness. But illness does not matter for institutions, any more than pregnancy matters or caring for someone else who is ill matters. Careers are not supposed to show gaps. When life is understood as a career, the résumé becomes an extension of the body. Gaps in the résumé are institutional stigmas. Since most of us have to work, it is hard for ill persons to resist accepting "productivity" as the measure of our worth.

In all these experiences people denied what I was going through or had been through, and the one medical resident who did not deny was told he should have. The sad logic of such denials is that the ill person ends up feeling guilty for the disease, the suffering, or the low productivity.

The ultimate denial is by friends and loved ones who simply disappear from the ill person's life. In disappearing, they deny that anything special is happening or, alternatively, that the ill person exists at all. Either form of denial can be truly devastating. If I asked these people why they disappeared from Cathie's life and mine during cancer, they would probably say they were busy, they did not want to bother us, and they "knew" we would call if we needed anything. But what we needed was to hear they cared. Such people can't see what their behavior looks like to the ill person and those who are caring for him or her. At Christmas, just after a chemotherapy treatment, I was at a small family gathering but was still too weak to get up and circulate among the guests. Someone I had felt close to arrived, a man I had not heard from during my illness. He did not come to the end of the room where I was sitting and did his best not to look in my direction. Perhaps I was too vulnerable to go to him or just too tired, or perhaps I felt, as I do now, that it was his responsibility to come to me.

A relative tried to excuse the behavior of some of the people who disappeared from Cathie's and my life during cancer by saying that they "cared silently at a distance." We know cancer is hard for people to confront, but from the perspective of the ill person and caregivers, "caring silently" might as well not be happening. Their distance looks like another denial of the illness. Just as I had expected that physicians would behave differently if I became critically ill, I also expected something more from family and friends. My expectations weren't always met; although the generous became more giving, the busy were still too busy.

Those who best affirmed my experience were often people who had been through critical illness themselves or with someone close. We did not necessarily talk a great deal about specific experiences, but these friends seemed able to look at me clearly and to accept what they saw. They rarely tried to cheer me up, but being with them usually did cheer me. Human suffering becomes bearable when we share it. When we know that someone recognizes our pain, we can let go of it. The power of recognition to reduce suffering cannot be explained, but it seems fundamental to our humanity.

People can recognize the experience of the ill in many ways. We needed the friends who called, brought food, sent cards, and took Cathie to lunch. They affirmed that we were still there and had needs. I write "we" because in many of these affirmations, as in many of the denials, an action toward me or toward Cathie affected the other one equally.

Cathie remains the caregiver whose affirmations mean the most to me. When it was becoming certain that I had cancer, she put her arms around me and told me she needed my survival, that her life required mine. I took the strength I needed from her and survived, but at a cost to her. Society organizes illness so that every demand is put on those who care for the ill. Someone is expected to get the patient to treatment, fill the prescriptions, notify friends and family of news, clean and supply the house, coordinate with the ill person's employer, change bandages and do other medical tasks at home, be a pleasant and loving visitor in the hospital, get the oil changed in the car, and ask the physician the questions the patient is too drugged to remember. Once during chemotherapy Cathie noticed that the nurse had reversed the suction on the intravenous pump, so that it was drawing blood rather than pumping in drugs. The responsibilities of the caregiver have no bounds.

But neither hospitals in particular nor society in general recognize or support the caregiver. Hospital spaces and schedules are designed to treat diseases; they do not accommodate people trying to sustain relationships while illness is tearing apart their lives. When medical staff need assistance, they expect the caregiver to be on call; otherwise he or she is a visitor. Medicine assumes that the person who has the disease is the only one who is ill. This assumption is shared by other institutions and even by family and friends, who should realize that illness is an experience that a couple has together — each differently, but one no less than the other.

I remember the night early in my illness when I looked in the mirror and thought of all I was going to lose before it was over. But I, we, did not realize that Cathie might lose even more. Few people who have not had a critical illness seem to recognize the danger and the losses to the caregiver. The notion of disease gave me some excuse for my absences from work; Cathie had as many added demands but none of the excuses. Some colleagues who praised her efforts caring for me and for her mother would then ask her for the work she was supposed to be doing during this time, the "real" work as opposed to the work of caring for others. The ill person has no choice but to give up status as a result of time "lost." The caregiver willingly accepts the personal costs of giving time and energy to the ill person. That most caregivers are women makes society's nonrecognition of caring a central cause of women's disadvantage in jobs and career advancement.

With luck, the ill person recovers. Recovery is a catharsis after chemotherapy; as the drugs left my body, I felt the rush of coming out of the cold and remembering what it was like to feel good. My recovery certainly had its doubts and fears, but I have never felt so ready for life's possibilities. The healing of the body can bring a healing of the mind. As much as I resented the demand that I make up for lost time, I was prepared to do so. But the caregiver's body experiences none of this. Can the pleasure she takes in watching the ill person recover give her the energy to make up for her own lost time? The person who was ill can speak of having lived through the disease; what the caregiver lived through is less easily expressed. Society has few terms to express the experience of caring, so it goes unrecognized.

But the problem is not just society. Cathie's greatest source of stress was me. She had to live each day with my fears, my obsession with this or that change in my condition, my bargaining over possible outcomes, my guilt and sense of rejection. Many of these problems were imposed on me, but the point is that they all came down on Cathie. Even she could be overpowered by my needs. It can be harder for the ill person to hold on to those who want to affirm than to ignore those who deny.

Being a caregiver is doubtless an opportunity, but the dangers of losing herself, her energies and appetites, and her sense of a future may be even greater for the caregiver than for the ill person. As little as we know of illness, we know even less of care. As much as the ill person's experience is denied, the caregiver's experience is denied more completely.

My good luck was to have a wife who was willing to be a caregiver. Together we sought to affirm the values of illness and caring that others, and sometimes even we ourselves, denied.

Comforters and Accusers

IN THE BIBLE, after Job has lost all his possessions, his children have been killed, and his skin has been covered "with sore boils from the sole of his foot unto his crown," his wife gets angry. "Curse God, and die," she tells him. Job refuses anger: "Shall we receive good at the hand of God, and shall we not receive evil?" he replies. If Job talked that way today, and if his misfortunes included cancer, he would be told he had a typical cancer personality.

Throughout this century theories have been advanced that the feelings people suppress, such as anger, cause them to have cancer. In the 1930s the poet W. H. Auden wrote a poem about Miss Gee, whose doctor attributed her cancer to childlessness and sexual repression. In the 1980s novelist Norman Mailer's fictional hero claimed he got cancer because one day he wasn't tough enough to keep chasing a gangster who had shot him. Cancer began the day he gave up on a fight, and it went into remission when he colluded in the murder of some other bad guys. Most of today's self-help authors are more subtle than Auden or Mailer, but they make the same claim that attitude causes cancer. Job's unwillingness to express his anger, to curse God, would be a prime example of someone whose personality caused cancer.

The specific makeup of the cancer personality varies. Sometimes it is based on too little sex or anger, other times on too much fear or frustration. For the last decade the suppression of anger has been more popular than sexual repression. Descriptions of cancer personalities are like horoscopes — broad enough to fit anyone, but just specific enough to allow individuals to believe their own lives are being described.

After Job's wife leaves him, he is visited by three friends whom he calls, with increasing irony, his comforters. Their comfort consists of blaming Job for having caused his own suffering. Sometimes this blame is subtle; other times it is overt: "If only you had directed your heart rightly and spread out your hands in prayer to him!" Job's friends appear as comforters, but they are really accusers. I understand them as extensions of Satan, who makes the wager with God to torment Job and see if he will renounce God. Recently "Satan" has been translated as "the Adversary" and "the Accuser."

Those who tell persons with cancer that their disease is caused by their personalities present themselves as comforters, but they too are accusers. The misfortune of getting cancer frightens people today as much as Job, who represented the complete reversal of fortune, frightened people in biblical times. Like the suddenness of Job's misfortunes, cancer represents how quickly lives can fall apart. We all fear that possibility; we want to be able to believe that we can avoid it, so we, like Job's accusers, blame it on the ill person. And we too call that blame comfort: cancer personality theories are presented as "self-help."

Society has always had personality theories to explain the

diseases it feared and did not understand. In one of the most sensible books ever written about cancer, *Illness as Metaphor,* Susan Sontag traces the history of such thinking to medieval times, when it was believed that happy people would not die of plague. We cannot prevent cancer any more than they could prevent plague, and we fear it as much. They claimed happiness was protection; we say people who do not repress anger or sex — or whatever is in fashion — will not get cancer.

We should find it funny when Sontag describes the ideas of the early psychoanalyst Wilhelm Reich, who wrote that Freud got cancer of the jaw because he repressed what he wanted to say. Because his repression involved speaking, his cancer was in the jaw. Auden placed Miss Gee's cancer, based on sexual repression, in her ovaries. But this kind of thinking is not funny, because it continues today.

A friend told me she had heard that breast cancer, which she had, was caused by problems in mother-daughter relationships. It was painful for her to think that her actions, with both her mother and her daughter, had caused her cancer. She turned the cancer personality into her own guilt, but the theory can be used against others. A woman told me that her boyfriend blamed the strains in their relationship for his cancer. Spouses or lovers may not always be supportive of someone who has cancer, but they do not cause it. Mothers may pass on a real genetic risk to their daughters, but again, relationships are not part of this risk.

When Job's accusers made him responsible for his misfortunes, they protected themselves from thinking that what had happened to him could happen to them. They, being righteous, would never end as Job had. Today the healthy want to believe that disease does not "just happen." They want to believe that they control their health and that they have earned it. Those who have cancer must have done something wrong, which the healthy can then avoid. The sick person must have participated in sickness by choosing to have a cancer personality. Otherwise illness is an intolerable reminder of how risky life is.

A friend called recently for advice about a man she knows who had just been diagnosed as having testicular cancer. She emphasized that until the diagnosis he had been absolutely fine. I wanted to say to her, Of course he was fine, disease does not always send early warning notices. But there was no need right then to remind her how fragile her world is. She is aware of that fragility in principle, but she is still shocked when a crack suddenly appears before her. Too many people find it easy to mend that crack by blaming its cause on the ill person. If we believe that the ill person has a cancer personality, then the world is less fragile, less risky, for everyone else. Even many ill people would rather believe they have done something wrong than believe disease just happened to them; guilt may be preferable to uncertainty.

For those who want to believe in a cancer personality, suppression of anger is an easy category to fit patients' behaviors into. Suppressed anger does not cause cancer, but being treated for cancer often requires the suppression of anger. One day I was lying in day care, waiting for blood results to come back from the lab. On the other side of the treatment area a physician was talking loudly with a volunteer, discussing vacation spots in the Caribbean, specifically, which side of some island was the rainy side. This was not a conversation I or the others having chemotherapy wanted to hear. Most of us were worried about getting through the day's treatment without having a vein collapse. We were wondering if we would ever leave Calgary again, much less get to a place like the Caribbean. Physicians need vacations, but these two never considered how they sounded to others; they failed to recognize what ill persons are living through.

In a chemotherapy unit, their talk was an appropriate object for anger. But Cathie and I kept our anger to ourselves, just as we had concealed our anger toward the physicians who misdiagnosed me. We grumbled only to ourselves because I was dependent on the treatment facility, and we were making our best deal.

Whether in treatment or at home, ill persons rarely perceive expressing anger as part of the best deal. Dependence is the primary fact of illness, and ill persons act with more or less fear of offending those they depend on. It seems like a bad deal to express anger at someone who may soon be approaching your body with sharp pointed instruments or, if offended, may be slow to bring a bedpan, or who may be the only person one can say goodnight to. Patients who do express anger usually believe they have little left to lose; the situation and the disease have already done their worst.

I did not need to have cancer to find myself in situations that made me angry. But when my treatment for cancer depended on suppressing my anger, when it was a matter of life and death, then the suppression was particularly bitter. And only as a person with cancer was I told that "my" suppression of anger had caused the disease in the first place.

Cancer personality theories will persist, because they have a payoff for everyone. On the one hand the ill person is accused, but on the other she is comforted. Perhaps by changing her personality she can recover; it is never too late. Those around the ill person can rest assured that he got cancer because he was that sort of person, different from themselves. Society as a whole can continue to perpetuate conditions and behaviors that increase the risks of cancer while blaming its incidence on the personalities of individuals. We can smoke, pollute, expose ourselves to radiation, use unsafe food additives, destroy the ozone layer, consume high levels of fat, take inadequately tested prescription drugs, make work more stressful, have an educational and occupational system that encourages delayed childbearing, fail to require retraining of physicians who make wrong diagnoses — but we still talk about causes of cancer in terms of individual personality.

The genius of the cancer personality argument is that it means nothing has to change. The fault and the fear are safely contained, locked up inside the cancer patient. Cigarette companies stay in business, polluters can pollute, advertisers can glorify sunbathing, and those who enjoy good health can believe they have earned it. Only the ill are left to feel guilty.

After Job has dismissed the arguments of his accusers, God answers him. The answer to his misfortune is that he has no right to ask. Job learns that his misfortunes are nothing more than part of his humanity. Job's final words, in Stephen Mitchell's translation, are, "Therefore I will be quiet, comforted that I am dust." Cancer is no god, but the person with cancer can find in Job's story a kind of answer and comfort. Disease is part of the dust of our bodies; we accept it when we accept life. It is our humanity to contest disease as long as we can, but it is also our humanity to die.

That is an answer to disease; illness is another problem.

One of the real tragedies of cancer is that so much anger is kept quiet. If expressed and responded to, this anger would make the world a better place. Having cancer taught me how many of the actions of individuals, institutions, and society are simply not decent ways to behave. When I was ill I expressed little of this anger, not because I had a cancer personality, but because I was doing what I had to do to get by. I write now for the times I had to remain silent and for those who are still silent.

Even when we are not forced into a deal requiring us to suppress anger, finding the appropriate object for anger is not easy. People, whether physicians, manufacturers, or smokers, act within systems they did not create. Getting angry at individuals does only so much good, but it does some good. Each friend, associate, or treatment provider remains responsible for his actions. We need to be angry with individuals who treat us badly, just as we need to appreciate all the obstacles society and its institutions use to prevent us from expressing this anger. Cancer personality theory is one such obstacle; it turns people inside themselves, into their own guilt, and away from changing the society that perpetuates real risks. The cancer personality theory is the final insult by comforters who are really accusers.

Valuing Illness

PHYSICIANS and nurses, medical ethicists and philosophers, economists and political scientists express opinions about what care society owes or does not owe ill persons. As an aging population combines with advancing medical technology, more people will need treatment, and more treatment will be available. The question is who will get what and who will pay. But in all that has been written, the ill themselves have had little to say, or else no one has listened. From the perspective of an ill person, the root issue is suffering. Is society willing to recognize the suffering of the ill as a common condition of humanity, and can we find value in illness? I believe that when society learns to value the ill, the other questions of rights — the complicated questions of payments and technologies and treatments — will fall into place with remarkable ease.

Seeing the question of rights from the perspective of the ill begins with accepting the inevitability of illness. To everyone except those who die in accidents or conflicts, a disease will just happen someday. That fact is not popular, and those who are not presently ill prefer to think about decreasing their risks of disease by living one way rather than another. We can decrease risks, and we should. But no amount of vitamins, proper diet, exercise, sunshine or sunscreen, relaxation, meditation, or joyful stress will change two facts: each of us will die, and most deaths will be preceded by a long or a short illness. I write this easily, based on an experience that was hard. When my mother-in-law was dying, she spent some time in the same hospital room where I had been treated not long before. It did not take much imagination to see myself in her place.

If those persons who are not presently ill could believe that disease is their inevitable fate, they might think differently about who pays for treatment. I have not mentioned costs and fees, and American readers may be puzzled by the omission. In Canada government insurance pays everyone's costs of medical care through general tax revenues. Physicians and treatment facilities remain autonomous, but instead of billing patients or insurance companies, they bill the province or receive provincial funding. The patient receives treatment just as she would in the American system, except that she gives the hospital or doctor her health-care identification number instead of making a payment. For all my treatments for heart problems and cancer, the only medical bill we paid was a fifteen-dollar-a-day surcharge for a private room I was assigned once by chance. This was later reimbursed by my university health insurance. We did pay for a small proportion of the prescription drugs I took at home to offset side effects of chemotherapy. Our only other expenses were for parking, and for Cathie's meals at the hospital.

The Canadian health system is being attacked by those who complain about its expense. In fact Canada spends a lower proportion of its gross national product on health care than the United States does. The cost, however, is distributed equally among all taxpayers rather than falling disproportionately on the ill. It is this distribution that is under attack. Some of those doing the attacking may want a system that allows them to use greater personal resources to purchase more exclusive treatment; others may want to open health care to entrepreneurial profit making. Still others may deny that someday they will need treatment, and want ill persons — others — to pay for what they get.

I can imagine nothing more cruel than being forced to make my own treatment decisions based on cost. As a minor example, the nurses at day care gave us the syringes we used every day to flush my intravenous line with saline solution. They told us that in other cancer centers the decision on how often to flush the line depends on the budget for syringes, not on what is most effective for maintaining the lines. They also told us that some lines fail because they are not flushed frequently enough. Given my dependence on the line, it would have been cruel to gamble on flushing it often enough. But in a system where patients themselves pay, it would be just as cruel to think that each time you flushed the line, you were taking resources away from your family. The strains an ill person imposes on family caregivers are great enough without depriving them financially as well.

Of course, private insurance provides treatment without the ill person having to pay for it directly. But private insurance is just that, available to some but not to all. There is nothing private about having cancer; I have never shared so self-consciously in the common risk of being human. Cancer may have been all I had in common with many of those in treatment with me, but cancer defined each of our lives. Because we shared cancer, I wanted no less for them than I wanted for myself. I did not want my treatment to be a privilege based on my occupation or income. If cancer occurs without prejudice, its treatment should be available without prejudice as well.

Even when treatment is publicly funded, it remains unequal. Depending on personal income, ill persons differ in their access to good nutrition, the restfulness of their home, their ability to reduce their workload, and even recreation. The effectiveness of treatment reflects these inequalities, but treatment itself should be a high-water mark of fairness. At least those who shared my disease had access to the same treatment I had. My recovery was not bought at the cost of anyone else's lack of treatment.

The right to treatment is the beginning of recognizing the ill, but it is not yet an expression of value. Even if society provides treatment to all, it may still relegate the ill to the margins where we drop off the other "unproductive" ones — children, the handicapped, the old, the untrained. Treatment in itself is not an expression that the individual is valued; it is an investment in the ill person's future productivity. The ill are regarded as healthy people inside broken-down bodies that need fixing. The hard question is whether we can value the ill as people whose experience challenges the way the rest of us live.

The healthy can begin to value illness by doubting the standard of productivity by which they measure their lives. Although I have once again become "productive," I am not sure if I am living better or worse than I was during illness. I often wish I could live a bit more as I did then, without having to have cancer. Illness, and perhaps only illness, gives us permission to slow down. It took a disease as devastating as cancer to allow me simply to sit and watch the afternoon light and finally think seriously about that picture of Jacob I had merely looked at for sixteen years.

I often think I have not yet been ill enough to know how to live. I still evaluate choices in terms of what counts on my résumé, instead of asking whether I am producing something I think is valuable and if I am meeting people's needs rather than fulfilling the demands of some system. I still feel threatened by the disease and the suffering of others. The threat is not only that I might become like them again, but that I might have to stop and care for someone else. I fear not only suffering but slowing down. It is natural to fear suffering; to fear slowing down is deranged. But all around me I see people afraid of slowing down, fearful of offending the production machines we work for.

Several years after chemotherapy, I now find myself resenting the time I spend on tasks I wanted so much to do, but lacked the strength for, when I was ill. I take my senses for granted, and I miss the joy I felt from suddenly hearing music or taking a walk or being in my own home and sleeping through the night. When I was ill I valued just being with others. Too often now I think of people as intruding on my work. I forget to ask myself if what I'm doing is so terribly important that I should allow it to crowd out all else.

Instead of setting the healthy and the ill apart, we should think about the rights of the living. Among the basic rights that should belong to every human is that of experiencing what is happening to oneself. We are so rushed from moment to moment that we are unable to reflect on what we are becoming. We spend our lives learning to be productive, to use our bodies as instruments of production. Whether we work at a computer terminal or on an assembly line or in a home, we know exactly what it means to use the body as an instrument of production. We know very little of what it means to be productive *of* ourselves, but this sort of production should be our basic human right.

To understand what the rights of the ill mean, we must ask what is required to produce one's self as a human being. This kind of production first requires care from others, and then it requires time, space, basic comforts, and some level of aesthetic choice. Ultimately it requires that the conditions of our lives enable us to return to others something of the care we have received. All this is necessary if we are to experience life rather than just survive it. None of these rights should be anything special.

The ultimate value of illness is that it teaches us the value of being alive; this is why the ill are not just charity cases, but a presence to be valued. Illness and, ultimately, death remind us of living. "The way we look to a distant constellation / That's dying in a corner of the sky," Paul Simon sang. We look like a flicker of light. In the moment of that light going out, we learn that what counts is to keep it burning. Death is no enemy of life; it restores our sense of the value of living. Illness restores the sense of proportion that is lost when we take life for granted. To learn about value and proportion we need to honor illness, and ultimately to honor death.

When my mother-in-law was dying, I found visiting her hard work. Cancer wards are not pleasant places, whether you bring the memories of an ex-patient or the anticipations of a possible future one. The demands of a working life provide easy excuses to stay away. But my mother-in-law had a right to the time of anyone she wanted to have around her. I had learned why when I lay in those same beds. Seeing the world from a bed in a cancer ward is like seeing it from outer space: it is rather small and fundamentally whole. To be ill, to share in the suffering of being human is to know your place in that whole, to know your connection with others. For the person who is dying, being with others expresses that connection, which alone has value and restores proportion.

My mother-in-law had no choice but to stay in that hospital, immobilized by breast, liver, and bone cancer, and experience her life running out. She had every right to whatever connection I could provide, but I had no less a right to my time with her. All I ever needed to learn about life was at her bedside in those days, shared in hearing her last words and watching the final struggles of her body. When our visits, and then her life, were over, I was able to walk outside under a blue or a starry sky, breathe real air, and know how we look to a distant constellation.

The rights of the ill resolve into the simplest questions. What is the core of experience that binds us together as human? If the answer includes suffering, then do we each, as individuals, have the strength to recognize our own place in that suffering? If we can recognize it, how do we honor it? These questions lead to the most practical ends: Is there any better reason to tax ourselves than for health care? What else do we have to do with our time than spend it with loved ones who are dying? The most practical question of all is how we can become productive of ourselves as human beings. We begin by witnessing the suffering of illness, sharing it, and allowing ourselves to live in the light of what that sharing teaches us we can be.

Listening to the Ill

ILLNESS excuses people from their normal responsibilities, but the cost of being excused is greater than it appears at first. An excuse is also an exclusion. When an ill person is told, "All you have to do is get well," he is also being told that all he *can* do is be ill. Telling someone he doesn't have to do anything but get well turns into a message that he has no right to do anything until he can return to his normal tasks. Again, just being ill has no value; on the contrary, the ill person is culpable.

People can't give up the idea that the ill person is responsible for the disease. If the ill person has a responsibility to get well, then presumably he is responsible for having become ill in the first place. The ideal of getting well also excludes and devalues those who will not get well.

Sad, but true

If we reject the notion that the ill are responsible for getting well, then what *is* their responsibility? It is to witness their own suffering and to express this experience so that the rest of us can learn from it. Of course others must be willing to learn; society's reciprocal responsibility is to see and hear what ill people express.

A recent newspaper story suggests how little we understand about the expression of experience as both a right and a responsibility. The story's theme is the need for cancer patients to "talk openly" about their illness. This need is defined as exclusively the patient's; the story does not mention society's need to hear such talk or whether others are willing to listen. The story, a medical-psychological moral fable, contrasts two teenagers with leukemia. One teenager exemplifies openness. When a stranger in a supermarket asks her if she is ill, she raises her wig and says that she is being treated for leukemia. The other teenager withdraws from friends and physicians and refuses further treatment. Without saying so, the article implies that the "open" child will survive and the "withdrawn" child will not.

takes a lot of courage

Stories like this perform a sleight of hand; they make the social context of each child's life disappear. Each teenager has a history of relationships with other people, and it is this history that produces the different behaviors. Their responses to leukemia do not just happen, the way some of us just happen to get leukemia. Whatever causes the disease, the response to it is learned. The teenagers' openness and withdrawal are responses to their experiences with family, friends, schools, and medical staff. The "open" one has been lucky enough to feel valued regardless of being ill. Her sense of stigma at home, at school, and in the hospital has been minimized. She has been allowed to feel that whatever problems her disease creates, illness is not a personal failure. She takes a risk when she shows her bald head to a stranger, but her willingness to do so results from how those around her have already responded to her baldness. The people she has met

she seems to feel comfortable with herself; hard to do when you have a critical illness

have acted in ways that allow her to anticipate support from those she now meets; at least she knows she has people to fall back on.

An ill child withdraws when he senses that people do not like what he represents. To his parents he embodies their failure to have a healthy child. He sees them being sad and guilty, and he feels guilty for having made them feel this way. To his siblings he may represent a drain on family time and financial resources. To other children his presence brings a fear of something they understand only enough to worry that it will happen to them. All adolescents experience their bodies changing, and his peers may see in the leukemic their fears of these changes gone wrong. To medical staff he represents their failure to cure him. I imagine his physicians evaluate their professional self-image in terms of the success of their treatments. They see themselves in a contest with the disease, and when disease persists, they have lost. They cannot think in terms of care that goes beyond treatment.

The child withdraws because he believes others would be happier if they did not have to see him. They may not reject him in any overt way, but he senses from their expressions that he is causing them pain. His withdrawal is no more the result of his "personality" (much less the lack of what some call "fighting spirit") than the other child's openness is. Each child is only looking around, assessing what support is available, and making what seems to be the best deal.

The newspaper story does not talk about the children's circumstances; instead it discusses withdrawal as "psychologically damaging" and openness as being "better adjusted." But the children are not damaged or adjusted; society is. The social group around each child has either helped her adjust or has damaged him, and those groups in turn find support or denial in other groups. The newspaper story makes these groups disappear through its use of the word "psychological," creating the illusion that each child's behavior comes out of that child, the way the leukemia comes from within the child's physiology. Healthy people comfortably accept the social myth that illness behavior is inside the person. We want to enclose the ill person in a psychological language that turns his reality inward, closing it off to external influence. Then we hand the whole thing over to medicine.

The ultimate moral of the story is medical compliance. The open child is the good medical citizen who stays in treatment. The withdrawn child plays his sick role badly. He does not try to get well. As soon as we think of the child's withdrawal as "his" and not a response learned from others, we cannot avoid the implication that he does not deserve to get well. Although the story quotes physicians and passes itself off as "scientific," the science only dresses up the moral fable beneath. The disease is depicted as a fall from the grace of a normal childhood. One child redeems herself through the courage of her openness, and the other continues falling. By making disease an issue of the ill person's morality, the story perpetuates a language of stigma.

Where is responsibility in this story? The newspaper account carries a clear implication that the ill person's responsibility is to be a good medical citizen. But the matter is not so simple. I see the children as equally responsible, though only one is happily so. The happy child lifts her wig and proclaims she is a leukemia patient. She performs a significant act of

[handwritten margin note: in addition, people believe that the open child is lucky, whereas the withdrawn one isn't]

public education, and I have no wish to detract from the honor she deserves. I hope the person she spoke to came away recognizing the ill person's strength as a person, not just a patient. When she perpetuates the openness she has experienced from others, the child widens the circle of public recognition. She has fulfilled her responsibility.

But the withdrawn child is no less responsible, no less a witness to his experience. Like the open child, he reflects the attitudes of those around him. He too acts according to others' cues of what they want of him, which is to disappear. His withdrawal may result in psychological damage, but again the initial damage is not the child's. The damage is caused by those who cannot value the ill.

[handwritten marginalia: Exactly. I totally agree.]

We may talk about the heroic individual who puts aside society's script for illness, but this is mostly just talk. Even the ill person who refuses to let her actions be determined by the way she is treated bases this response on resources developed earlier. Adolescents are more susceptible to the way they are treated at the moment because their personal history is shorter. We who are older are no less creatures of the ways we have been treated; we just have a longer history against which to evaluate our present circumstances.

The responsibility of the ill, then, is not to get well but to express their illness well. And the two have nothing to do with each other. I wish I could believe that those who express their illness well have a greater chance of recovery, but I cannot. Perhaps someday we will understand more of how the mind affects the body. For now I only believe that those who express their illness live their lives fully to the end of the illness. For me this is enough — it has to be enough. If we cannot value life for itself, then we see ill persons only in terms of what they could be doing if they were well, and we see children only as what they will do when they become adults. We fail to value life as a frail bit of good luck in a world based on chance.

The ill have already fulfilled their responsibility by being ill. The question is whether the rest of us can be responsible enough to see and hear what illness is, which ultimately means seeing and hearing what life is. Being alive is a dual responsibility: to our shared frailty, on the one hand, and to all we can create, on the other. The mutual responsibilities of the ill to express and the healthy to hear meet in the recognition that our creativity depends on our frailty. Life without illness would not just be incomplete, it would be impossible. The paradox is that illness must remain painful, even to those who fully believe its necessity.

The most painful sight we ever confront is that of beauty yielding to impermanence. Of our creations, we may consider children the most beautiful. When they reveal their frail impermanence by becoming critically ill, it is painful to remain open to that illness. In children most of all we want to deny illness. We want to withdraw into an illusion of permanence, that children will turn into adults, and we will not have to see them die. But that illusion is another sleight of hand in which life, the creative frailty and the frail creativity, disappears.

Ceremonies of Recovery

RECOVERY deserves a ceremony. Many aboriginal peoples have reentry rituals during which a person who has been stigmatized is purified. These rituals are a rebirth; afterward life can begin anew. Each of my critical illnesses ended with a medical event that could have been given a ritual value. But physicians, the high priests of our time, have let themselves be reduced to mere medical technicians. They act as if they are unaware of the power of their interventions to change the body's symbolic value. Both the patient and physician are thus deprived of the spiritual experience of illness. Because ritual self-awareness is excluded from the system, it takes longer to work out one's own terms of reentry.

The angiogram which showed that my heart problems were over had ritual potential, and I had the sense to value the sight of my own heart beating. But medicine reduced the angiogram to the end of an incident. I accepted, even embraced, this reduction and did not try to experience it as the beginning of a life that was now different. The angiogram only signaled the end of a breakdown; it was not an occasion for rebirth.

After the angiogram I could believe that the incident was over. There had been a virus, but now it was gone. I had no more heart problems, period. After cancer, however, I had no such belief. Cancer never disappears. I read recently about a young man whose cancer recurred after a thirteen-year remission. Medical science is just beginning to understand cancer's capacity to be present in the body but inactive for decades. Cancer creates the disturbing image of the body as a time bomb, genetically programmed to explode at some future time. I could be having a recurrence now and not yet know it, or I could live another forty years and die of something else. You are never cured of cancer; you can only live in remission.

My remission began several weeks after the third round of chemotherapy. The CAT scan showed that the tumors had shrunk, but the reduction was no longer considerable. The remaining masses on the X-rays were assumed to be scar tissue, which would never disappear entirely but would continue to reduce gradually. The chemotherapy was judged to have done what it could. My treatment could end.

My intravenous line provided its last valuable service as the occasion of a ceremony. After reporting the scan, the physician left Cathie and me in a treatment cubicle while he prepared another room for the surgical procedure of pulling out the line. Its installation had changed our relationship by requiring each of our days to begin and end with a focus on cancer. The care of the line had tied Cathie to me and tied us both to cancer; these ties had brought nuisance and caring, fear and possibility. Because of the line's symbolism, as well as its problems, we had looked forward to its removal as the beginning of life after cancer. My own emotions were intensified by the physical drain of preparing for the scan. I had not eaten in about twenty-four hours and had had almost no sleep. My physical reserves and our emotional reserves were gone, so we started to cry, in a mixture of joy, relief, and just plain breakdown.

When a nurse came into the room and saw us crying, she looked totally confused. Suddenly a light bulb went on. "I guess this must be kind of a big moment for you," she said. She was a good nurse and had been mercifully quick and efficient at getting prescriptions to manage painful side effects, but for her, suffering was a problem of management, not a crisis of spirit. Her perceptions were always on the surface of bodies. That moment was one of the few times she saw beyond the disease to the experience of illness. She talked happily of former patients returning to see her when their hair had grown back; chemotherapy sounded like a problem of grooming. When hair returns, all is forgotten. But when all is forgotten, nothing is learned. Her way of seeing missed the ritual, which is a passage through real and symbolic dangers in preparation for the opportunity of a life enhanced by that passage.

The line was pulled, the incision sewed up. Medicine, as ritual, inflicted another mark on my body, giving that body a value it did not have before. Ritual markings are not just stigmas; scarification during an initiation rite marks the person as having passed through some level of experience, entitling him to higher status as a result. Thus initiated, my body was mine again. Life could begin once more. Of course I knew life had never stopped. The nights listening to Bach, the afternoon light on the Chagall print, the moments of hope and fear shared with Cathie, the losses and frustrations had been anything but life stopping during cancer. It had only intensified. If the months from the ultrasound in September to the removal of the line in January seemed like a lifetime, it was because during this time everything counted. I could not afford to let anything slip by unobserved and unfelt.

My life had not stopped, but a great deal of it had been put on hold. Now I could begin to make plans again, to think of travel, to commit myself to projects at work. The process of reentry was not smooth. I now knew that the way I and others lived was a choice, and often not the best one. My consciousness remained suspended between the insulated world of illness and the "healthy" mainstream. This suspension expressed itself in my lack of tolerance for tension and disagreements. I continued to value much of the life of an ill person, even though I was no longer officially diseased.

I still needed time to myself. It was warm in Calgary that winter, and I took long walks on the hills overlooking the river. I chose the time for these walks so that I would come over the crest of the hill just as the afternoon sun shone directly on the water. Chemotherapy had deprived me of air and sun. I wanted to store up these elements against the possibility that I might be deprived of them again. In that sunlight on the river I began to heal.

I become less and less a person with cancer, but the continuing schedule of examinations, X-rays, and blood tests reminds me that I remain at greater risk than others. This risk diminishes over time but never disappears. Life remains a remission. But my sense of being a person with cancer is on the level of experience, not of medicine. I do not want to take recovery too far. Part of the fear of dying is realizing all that

[handwritten marginal note:] illness can lead you to discover the value of life, which I believe, you can never forget after you're "healthy"

I have not done or have not done enough of. As long as life remains a recovery, I try to seize the life I someday want to have lived. The value of remaining a person with cancer is to keep asking the question: If I get sick again, what will I tell myself about the way I spent my time?

I am also reminded of cancer when I meet people I see infrequently. Some ask, guardedly, how my health is. Their concern recognizes that cancer is never "over" in the way a virus is over when it passes out of the body. Others greet me by pronouncing, "You're fine." Theirs is less a question than a statement. I hear their wish that cancer never happens, and, if it has to happen, that it be put away. I have assumed a dual presence for people. My being here suggests that cancer is not always fatal, but that it does happen. Some see the survival in the foreground and the risk in the background; for others the risk dominates. On different days I myself emphasize different halves.

[handwritten margin note: personally, I would relate to this statement]

I am trying, in this third year after cancer, to be a little less afraid. Some days the world seems immensely fearful, a place where some germ cell is waiting to explode. Another of Paul Simon's memorable lyrics says, "Somebody could walk into this room / And say your life is on fire." One day during a self-examination I felt something I had not felt in the two years since surgery. I panicked but made an appointment to see the same urologist who had originally diagnosed me. A few days later Cathie and I were again waiting in a treatment ward, listening to the other patients through the thin curtains. We sat there waiting for the urologist, who could walk into that room and say our lives were on fire. But it did not happen that time. Whatever it was I had noticed, he pronounced me normal. We left, less happy than dazed by the vision of what might have happened. This vision gives each day its value. Of course the condition of my life is no different from anyone else's, but I get these reminders, for which I am grateful.

The only real difference between people is not health or illness but the way each holds onto a sense of value in life. When I feel I have no time to walk out and watch the sunlight on the river, my recovery has gone too far. A little fear is all right. It is all right to know that in a month I could be lying in a hospital bed asking myself how I spent today. Holding onto that question — how did you spend today? — reminds me to feel and see and hear. It is too easy to become distracted. *exactly;* → When the ordinary becomes frustrating, I have to remember *don't take* those times when the ordinary was forbidden to me. When I *things for* was ill, all I wanted was to get back into the ordinary flux of *granted)* activity. Now that I am back in the ordinary, I have to retain a sense of wonder at being here.

Like Job, I have had my goods restored to me. Secure in the knowledge that I am dust, I enjoy what I have. I even run again, not as far or as fast, but with greater pleasure. Long runs let my mind drift to whatever fantasy comes along. Some days that fantasy turns to my death, but not in sadness. I wonder what kind of death I would need, to feel I had lived well. What I tell myself changes; all that matters is staying at peace with my own mortality.

I want to keep running, but someday I will have to stop. I do not know what that day will be like. If I have recovered well but not too much, I will remember a poem I keep over my desk by the late Raymond Carver, called "Gravy." A man, an alcoholic, is about to die, but he changes his habits and lives for ten years. Then he gets a brain disease and again is dying. He tells his friends not to mourn:

> "I've had ten years longer than I or anyone
> expected. Pure gravy. And don't you forget it."

I try not to.

When I become ill again, and someday I will, I hope it will not be the total break in my life, the radical discontinuity, that I experienced before. Health and illness are not so different. In the best moments of my illnesses I have been most whole. In the worst moments of my health I am sick. Where should I live? Health and illness, wellness and sickness perpetually alternate as foreground and background. Each exists only because of the other and can only alternate with its other. There is no rest in either word. In "health" there can only be fear of illness, and in "illness" there is only discontent at not being healthy. In recovery I seek not health but a word that has no opposite, a word that just is, in itself. When I seek the meaning of my recovery, the opportunity of illness, I call it gravy.

[handwritten margin note: you have to face reality, just don't let it make you paranoid or depressing. Take each day as it is and live life to its fullest.]

Gravy

I BEGAN THINKING about the experience of illness when I recognized something of my own situation in the picture of Jacob wrestling with the angel. I can end my story with this morning's "Far Side" cartoon. A bearded man stands at the front door, dripping wet, in rags. The woman opening the door says, "For crying out loud, Jonah! Three days late, covered with slime, and smelling like a fish! . . . And what story have I got to swallow this time?" Like Jonah, I have been spit back into life by the great fish of illness. The story I have been asking you to swallow is almost over.

Our lives are attempts to make sense of what we are living through. Self-reflection is our curse and our possibility. I have suggested that illness is an opportunity for self-reflection of a kind not otherwise available. This opportunity has its dangers, not the least of which is romanticizing illness. We need to think about illness, but too much thinking can turn it into something it is not. Illness is not any kind of enlightenment. Illness is nothing more than the body moving on. My body was moving too rapidly toward death. Surgery and chemicals restored that movement to its normal pace, sort of. Some part of me still knows where it was going. I wait to finish the journey my body now knows is inescapable. I hope to wait a long time, but not forever.

I have written little of death because I have little to say. At the same time I was diagnosed as having cancer, a good friend my age was also diagnosed, and my mother-in-law came out of remission again. They both have died. I can make no sense of their deaths and my survival. Some people who have lived through cancer attribute their survival to some act of will. They speak of choosing to live and of the mind willing the body back to health. They mean well, and their belief may bring comfort to some. But when I think of the real people who are now dead, and wonder why I live, the idea that I chose to live and they did not seems presumptuous at best and obscene at worst. Disease just happened to them in the same way it just happened to me. It just happened to happen differently.

Sometimes I feel very strange, just being alive. It's a comfortable strangeness, but strange nonetheless. My body seems to know in some way that it should not be living. Just as my body remembers the moment of death during my heart attack, it knows it was dying of cancer and cannot figure out what stopped the process. I happened to get cancer, and then I happened to respond to a treatment that happened to be available. That's the strangeness of contingency: neither my body nor my mind knows why these things happened as they did. As I remake my place in this life, it too seems to have just happened, to be a contingency.

But if disease just happens, where does choice fit in? People who have died are often described as "cancer victims." This phrase has a certain accuracy, but it eliminates the choice that was also theirs. The word "victim" is a half-truth. We may be victims of disease, but we are not victims of illness. Individuals can do little to prevent certain diseases. If many people choose to act in certain ways, those choices, spread across a population, will change the total incidence of disease. Such action matters when we consider a whole society, but for any individual, odds are only odds. Some of those with the lowest risk factors will still get sick, and in some sense, though only in part, they will be victims.

Choice becomes possible when we shift the perspective from the disease to the illness. Because we can choose how we experience illness, we can be more than victims. Choice can turn the worst of circumstances into an experience of value. But choices are limited. The care I received was my good luck, not my choice. We can choose only from what is available. We are not victims of circumstances, but circumstances limit our choices. The idea of choice is another half-truth. The trick is to hold onto the half that is true.

I used to think of activities like running and writing as choices. Then cancer prevented me from doing them, and I decided they were gifts. But gifts imply a giver. Now I think that much of what happens just happens. One day you run twenty miles and the next you have a heart attack. The gift is our human capacity to choose how we use each day, however limited our choices.

Half-victims making half-choices are my fellow citizens in the remission society. I began to think of myself as living in the "remission society" when I realized the ordinariness of my experience of illness. As I write and talk about illness, people tell me about living in some kind of remission, many from cancer, others from equally debilitating diseases. My history is nothing special.

The remission society is new. Disease used to be either critical, meaning life-threatening but quick, or chronic, meaning long-term. Disease moved to a crisis from which the patient either recovered or died, or else the patient lived as an invalid, gradually wasting away. Medical technology keeps enlarging the numbers of those living "normally" in remission; we have more and more of the "chronically critical." They go about their business with alternating periods of activity and treatment. Life for them is remission, as it is for their caregivers. By choosing to tie their lives to the illness of others, caregivers too see life as a kind of remission. They too know that somebody could walk into the room and say their lives are on fire.

What is life like in the remission society? For me it is ordinary or everyday, a quality so simple and so everpresent that it becomes difficult to describe. The quality of light in a room is everyday, as is the smell of the air. Being among people is ordinary; so are clothes we like, food we enjoy, and the fit of a body into a comfortable chair, the touch of other bodies. These details make up any life. People in the remission society notice details more, because illness teaches the value as well as the danger of the everyday.

The danger is that ordinary discomforts will persist and accumulate. I have written of many discomforts that in the course of a healthy life would be no more than annoying: morning blood tests in the hospital, strong laxatives before

CAT scans, and even any single side effect of chemotherapy. But as these mundane discomforts accumulate, they take over everyday life. They become all an ill person has to look forward to. And one day, after many days with nothing else to look forward to, that person changes. She doesn't decide to change or even perceive that she has changed, but she has. She has been worn away, and she doesn't care anymore. Among caregivers this change is called burnout. Ill persons also burn out. Some may continue in treatment, but only because they don't care enough to stop. Those who do stop treatment are the ones who still care about how they live; they are willing to live a shorter time, under circumstances they hope will be more of their own choosing. The burned-out ones have given up caring. They keep going but are only waiting for the end.

But living among the everyday is also the opportunity of illness, which brings me back to gravy. Gravy is beyond health or illness, beyond the desire for health, which necessarily brings the fear of the illness. Gravy does not romanticize illness but is willing to accept it for what it can bring.

Gravy is watching the sunlight on the river. Here is half of what I have learned from illness:

> Sky is blue,
> Water sparkles.

This verse is only half. Watching the sunlight remains solitary. The other half of life's joys are with others, in pleasure and in pain. These halves become a whole. To be able to recognize the pain of others, to witness life's sufferings, we need some grounding in what is our own. My grounding is, Sky is blue, Water sparkles. From there I can begin to reach out.

[handwritten margin note:] I never thought of it that way. I always took the opposite, but I agree with this statement

The world I reach out to is a world in which I see myself. That was what I saw that night, early in my cancer, when I was in such pain. In that frosted window I saw myself. Not the self I see in a mirror, but a world I am so completely a part of that it too is myself. The sight allowed me to exist outside my body's pain and at the same time to see why that pain was part of the same world as the window, as necessary to that world as the window's beauty was. The lesson I learned looking into that frosted window was expressed centuries ago in the Chinese holy book, the *Tao Te Ching*:

> See the world as your self.
> Have faith in the way things are.
> Love the world as your self;
> then you can care for all things.

When I can care for the sunlight on the river enough to imagine that it will be there without me, when I have faith in its being there, then my self rests in a world beyond itself and I am no longer afraid to die. When I can see the faces of those I love smiling after I am gone, then I can take pleasure in being here. But I do not have to be here; my pleasure is knowing I can let go.

So the sun rises on another day in the remission society. It rises on a world that is everyday, in all its opportunity and danger. It rises on a day when some will be victims, and all will make choices, though some will have more scope for choice than others. In the remission society all struggle to be responsible, but only some will be granted the rights necessary to act in ways that enhance their lives. Many will experience stigma, a few will know it for what it is, and even fewer will be able to overcome how it makes them feel. Some will express anger, bits of which will find their proper target and lead someone else to change. Ill persons will be denied and will find care. Some will lie in rooms where they cannot see the sun, and others will find themselves at home, able to value it as they never have. Some will burn out; others will prevail.

How strange and wonderful the world must have looked to Jonah, come out of the belly of that great fish. Could he preserve the poignancy of that first moment, after three days in the slime and the stink, when he saw the light and land and water, and knew the face of God?

Throughout this book I have minimized the use of quotations and references to others' writings. But ideas do not derive from personal experience alone, and acknowledgment of works I have drawn on directly is due. Susan Sontag's *Illness as Metaphor* (Farrar, Straus and Giroux, 1978) taught me how careful ill persons must be in describing their illnesses, as well as in accepting descriptions from others. Arthur Kleinman's *The Illness Narratives* (Basic Books, 1988) affirmed the value of witnessing suffering. At a time when I was wondering whether to write this book, Kleinman's book showed me why ill persons need to express what they are going through, both for themselves and for the healthy.

My models of accounts by ill persons included two works by other social scientists: Irving Zola's *Missing Pieces* (Temple University Press, 1982) and Robert F. Murphy's *The Body Silent* (Henry Holt, 1987). Oliver Sacks's *A Leg to Stand On* (Harper & Row, 1984), Nan Shin's *Diary of a Zen Nun: Every Day Living* (E. P. Dutton, 1986), and John Updike's essay "At War with My Skin," in *Self-Consciousness: Mem-*

oirs (Ballantine, 1989), contained further lessons both on how to live with illness and how to turn it into narrative.

Although this book is not a work of sociology, I owe debts in that field also. Few nonspecialists may want to attempt the writings of Talcott Parsons, but his conception of "the sick role" has led me into my most productive disagreements. Parsons wrote about sickness in various books, from *The Social System* (Free Press, 1951) to *Action Theory and the Human Condition* (Free Press, 1978). Arlie Hochschild does not write about illness in *The Managed Heart* (University of California Press, 1983), but this book gave me a vocabulary to express my ideas about how ill persons are supposed to sustain an appearance acceptable to others. The one sociology book I would recommend to anyone is Erving Goffman's *Stigma* (Prentice Hall, 1963). Although Goffman says little if anything about cancer, his discussion of other "spoiled identities" applies in varying degrees to all ill persons.

Illness, as I have tried to write, presents us with many windows and mirrors. What I saw in them was affected most by works of poetry and spirituality. The writings of the Zen master D. T. Suzuki have informed my thinking thoughout. I also owe a singular debt to Stephen Mitchell for his translations of Rainer Maria Rilke's *Letters to a Young Poet* (Random House, 1984), the *Tao Te Ching* (Harper & Row, 1988), and *The Book of Job* (North Point Press, 1987), as well as his own commentaries and poetry. Compared to what these writings offer, what I have learned is nothing. But part of what they teach me is not to fear beginnings.